Jerry,
I respect you as a leader who leads
with integrity of heart and skillful hands.
I am a better leader because of you.

Mel

EFFECTIVE STAFFING
FOR VITAL CHURCHES

The
E S S E N T I A L   G U I D E
to Finding and Keeping the Right People

Bill Easum AND Bill Tenny-Brittian

BakerBooks
a division of Baker Publishing Group
Grand Rapids, Michigan

Published by Baker Books
a division of Baker Publishing Group
P.O. Box 6287, Grand Rapids, MI 49516-6287
www.bakerbooks.com

Printed in the United States of America

Library of Congress Cataloging-in-Publication Data
Easum, William M., 1939–
    Effective staffing for vital churches : the essential guide to finding and keeping the right people / Bill Easum and Bill Tenny-Brittian
        p.   cm.
    Includes bibliographical references (p.   ).
    ISBN 978-0-8010-1490-1 (pbk.)
    1. Church personnel management. I. Tenny-Brittian, William. II. Title.
BV652.13.E27 2012
254—dc23   2012023262

Published in association with the literary agency of Mark Sweeney & Associates, Bonita Springs, Florida, 34135

12 13 14 15 16 17 18   7 6 5 4 3 2 1

Contents

Foreword

When people look at struggling churches and the decline of self-identified Christians in America, a multitude of theories as to why this is happening and how the trends can be reversed are created. As a researcher, I can testify to the reality of these trends and the concern they cause among pastors and leaders whose hearts beat to see a genuine movement of God in North America. Long-term downward trends are very difficult to arrest, let alone turn around, yet I remain hopeful.

Much of the discussion surrounding how to reach unbelievers has focused around the "missional vs. attractional" debate, which is a needed conversation. In this book, however, Bill Easum and Bill Tenny-Brittian remind us of an often overlooked point: wise churches will pay close attention to staffing as it relates to their effectiveness. If the question "Does church staffing look different now than before?" is self-evident, then the question "How do we do staffing now?" surely is not. And the wrong answer will prove disastrous.

A long-accepted paradigm for staffing is that churches hire for each major ministry. The result is oftentimes a church that is top-heavy on payroll, with staff members working to justify their own existence. Such a situation makes it almost impossible for a church to maintain an outward focus since so much time, energy, and money are needed to maintain the infrastructure.

Understanding the process of hiring church staff is just as important now as it has ever been. Financial constraints, the changing North American mission field, and personnel shortages conspire to make the task of hiring effective staff a real challenge. When Jim Collins observed in *Good to Great* the necessity of businesses having the wrong people off the bus, the right people on the bus, and the right people in the right seats, he could have been speaking directly to churches in the twenty-first century. In a similarly colorful analogy, Easum and Tenny-Brittian write: "Our favorite way of describing the effects one ineffective staff person can have on the entire staff is to think of a stagecoach being pulled by eight horses in full gallop—and one of the horses decides to sit down" (p. 27).

The new realities of our post-9/11, post-Great Recession, and post-postmodern world of ministry is that we have less margin for staffing mistakes. Strategic hiring is crucial for the mission of the church. Decisions about which positions to create and when to create them are just as important as who will ultimately fill them. When should a church move from volunteers to paid staff in a particular area of ministry? In what order should staff positions be created and filled? Thankfully, the authors do not limit their writing to theoretical or ethereal discussions about what should be versus what is. They include plenty of practical implementation for the "How" questions that will inevitably arise.

Ahead in this book, you will read the authors' assertion that all effective churches are actually missional churches, and their argument that the church at Antioch is the best model for emulation. Even though the church in Jerusalem usually gets the lion's share of pastoral and seminary attention, they stress that studying the Antioch church will help us to better understand leadership today. These are bold statements, to be sure, but ones that need to be considered if we are to break out of the evangelistic malaise currently enveloping the church in North America.

The current struggles we face in no way stifle God's plan for his church, but it would still be foolish to ignore our drastically changing culture and not review our ministry strategies. The sons of Issachar, it is worth remembering, understood their times *and* knew what Israel should do (see 1 Chron. 12:32). We pay them no heed at all if we assume to know what the church should do *without* understanding the times. This book will help us do both.

Ed Stetzer, president of LifeWay Research
and coauthor of *Comeback Churches*

Introduction

Why Read This Book

With so many church books to choose from, it's reasonable to ask, "Why should I purchase this book?" Money is scarce, the cost of books is escalating, and there are more new books being published than ever before. We know this makes folks especially particular about which books they purchase. As pastors and consultants for several decades, we clearly see four reasons to pick up this one.

One: Money's Tight and Having the Right Staff Is Critical

In most churches the largest share of the annual budget goes to staff salaries. In recent history churches have largely depended on their staff to get congregational ministries up and running. Virtually every church we work with confesses to having a laity leadership vacuum and asks us how to get the most from the staff they have. A misstep in hiring and supervising staff isn't just expensive—it can be a congregational disaster.

Effective churches make the right staff choices. They have a supervision process that encourages growth and maturity. They know the difference between a player and a competent leader. Helping churches make efficient and effective staff choices is our underlying theme from the first page to the last.

Two: The Mission Field Has Changed

In the eyes of global Christianity, the United States is one of the largest mission fields in the world. Indeed, with the increase of immigration and diaspora of ethnicities from urban centers across the country, most communities can attest that the "world" has come to them. Add to that the rapid growth of the unchurched population and we're faced with a game-changer for everything the church does, including how a church is staffed.

However, staffing for today's church is only half the story. What about tomorrow's church? Although we don't profess to know your congregation's future, throughout this book we'll help you lay a foundation that will get you ready to face whatever comes.

Three: There's a Shortage of Leaders

Contrary to what some have predicted, we believe the local church will continue to need paid, skilled, and gifted leaders to lead the church. But we agree that the role of unpaid and volunteer church leaders is becoming increasingly important. However, by now everyone should be aware that the available pool of church leaders is shrinking each year. There are fewer men and women entering seminary, graduating, and remaining in the congregational ministry than any time in recent memory. And it's common knowledge that the number of people attending local churches has been in decline for decades.

As the pool of leaders dwindles, the chance of having or being a competent pastor or staff member declines proportionately. The key question that runs throughout this book is: Can today's average pastor, staff, and volunteer become tomorrow's exceptional leaders? We believe the answer is "Yes!"

Four: The Right Staffing Facilitates Church Growth

If you've been around the church block once or twice, you already know what the wrong staffing decisions can do to a church. Never mind the waste of resources; a bad hire can rip a congregation asunder and even lead to the church's demise. But what many church leaders don't realize is that the right hires can facilitate a sustainable growth culture.

Whether you're a leader in a church of 25 or 2,500, your next staffing decision has the potential to make you . . . or literally to break you. We've provided the technicalities of who, how, and why to make your next staffing choice for any size church—and the church you'll become.

One last thing. We've each shared personal stories and experiences throughout the book to help illustrate both what works and what doesn't work. Comments that apply to Bill Easum are marked with (BE) and those that apply to Bill Tenny-Brittian with (BTB).

1

Every Church Is Missional, or It Isn't a Church

Originally the title of this book was *Staffing the Missional Church*. However, we decided against that title for three reasons:

1. We believe every church is missional, or it isn't a church! But we use the word a bit differently than most books written on the missional church. We believe every true church is focused more on transforming the world than on building up its own membership. We subscribe more to the type of ministry seen in the Antioch church than to the ministry of the Jerusalem church. The Antioch church was focused outward on the world, whereas the Jerusalem church was more focused on itself and how to care for its people.
2. We also believe churches that sit around waiting for people to come to them have stopped being a church, and that such a purely attractional[1] church has no validity on a mission field.
3. Finally, we believe a church can be a church with or without a building. The church isn't about buildings—it's about people. So we reject the longstanding exercise taught to children,

We refuse to adopt the typical usage of the word missional *since we feel the word applies to every faithful and effective church.*

"Here's the church; here's the steeple; look inside and see all the people."

Throughout the book you will overhear bits and pieces of the missional/attractional conversations going on today. But we refuse to adopt the typical usage of the word *missional* since we feel the word applies to every faithful and effective church. So we will occasionally use the words *attractional* and *missional* because they so adequately show the difference between the ineffective and effective church today.

So join us now on a journey of growth—yours, the kingdom's, your church's, and your people's.

2

The Context for Everything

The emerging new world is changing everything, including how a church staff functions. Consider the following game-changers affecting every congregation and its staff.

People don't come to church on their own anymore. Now they must be brought by a friend, relative, neighbor, or co-worker. This is one of the most profound changes for Christianity in our lifetime.

When people do show up at church they are blank slates we must write on. In the past the majority of children in the United States either grew up in church, knew someone who did, or had at least some secondhand knowledge of what happens "at church." No more. Once upon a time the faith was both taught and modeled for children at home, at church, and even in school. We all know that doesn't happen today. Now it takes longer and requires more staff to disciple a person than it did two decades ago.

When people think of Christians and church they are skeptical about our motives. In the past pastors were revered even by people who didn't attend worship. No more. Now before we can disciple someone we have to gain their trust.

People are defecting from the church in record numbers. In the past adults remained in church after their children went off to college. No more. Today, parents are more apt to leave the church when their kids leave home than they are to remain in the church. That's why most effective churches focus much of their attention on the adults.

Global migration is changing demographics and culture. Between 1960 and 2000 the number of immigrants rose to 3 percent of the total population of developing countries. Yet the United States alone accounts for 20 percent of the world's immigrants, totaling more than 38 million people or almost 13 percent of the US population. Many of these immigrants are coming from some of the least reached groups of people.[1] In the near future if a church isn't multicultural it probably won't be growing—a profound effect on how a church is staffed.

The Result

Fewer people are attending worship today than ever before in the history of Western civilization, and when they do attend they are mostly clueless about what it means to be Christian.[2] Each decade the percentage of people attending worship drops.[3] Although Gallup still reports that about 79 percent of the US population consider themselves "Christian," these same polls also report that only 30 percent of the US population attend church regularly. In reality, even that 30 percent statistic is inflated. The fact is last weekend less than 17 percent of the US population graced the doors of a local congregation.[4] In the eyes of the world, the United States is seen as one of the largest mission fields in the world. Thus Christians who share their faith will be more like backyard missionaries than they would like to think.

The Game Has Changed

They don't come to us anymore. We must go to them.

These changes have enormous implications for the way a church staffs and functions. Because people no longer come to church on their own, the church must spend most of its time, energy, and money filtering people out into the community. The measurement of effectiveness shifts from "How many in worship?" to "How much difference is the church making in its efforts to transform the city?" The question "What is God doing in our community that we can be part of?" is replacing "How can we get more people to come to church?"

Today's church must think *outward* rather than *inward*. Instead of doing programs in the church building designed to keep the members active, staff must make preparing disciples to go out into the world as backyard missionaries their primary role. If the church is going to adapt to the sea of changes underway, it has to be and think and become *mission*.

In the effective church staff members function more as scouts and coaches than as doers of ministry. The smaller a church, the more time its pastor must spend in the community rather than in the office or with church members. The larger the church becomes, the more likely it is to have a staff person whose primary responsibility is to discover and implement ministries in the community instead of in the church building. But in any size church both the pastor and the staff's primary role is to provide a culture where people naturally connect with the unchurched.

Blank slates must be written on.

Because people come to church as skeptical blank slates, discipleship and leadership development become more important than programs and courses designed to keep people involved and active in the church. Unless a skeptical blank slate is written on by a transformative experience with Jesus Christ, all the programs in the world will not keep that person connected to the body of Christ.

As a result of these changes, on-the-job ministry and coaching replaces in-church programs and courses. As we've said many times, "*We* are the curriculum." They must see Jesus in us and in our actions. Although courses and programs that help disciple the unchurched can be used, they are no longer the primary thrust of evangelism.

Living on a Mission Field Changes the Kind of Staff Needed

If it's true, and we believe it is, that we now live in one of the world's biggest mission fields, then that must have a bearing on the kind of people we choose to lead our churches. Not just any staff

We have to listen to their story before we can tell them our story on the way to the story.

can step outside the walls of the institution and walk with Jesus on the road to mission. Not just any staff has a heart for people who haven't yet been transformed by Jesus. Not just any staff understands that it's not about them, but rather about submission to Christ. Not just any staff can internalize that it's all about the kingdom of God rather than growing a church. Finding the caliber of person to staff an effective church takes more than just looking through a few résumés or denominationally formatted "papers."

Living on a Mission Field Changes How a Staff Functions

Staffing an effective church is different than staffing the typical church of the past. It used to be most churches staffed primarily for the care and feeding of their members, and if any time was left over staff could attempt to reach out to the community. But even then church leaders looked for effective and innovative ways to proclaim, "Here we are; y'all come." Not so today.

Today the primary focus of an effective staff is the mobilization and empowerment of the entire congregation for the purpose of transforming the surrounding community and the world, which does result in the growth of the church as a by-product. This is a more "we have to go to them and meet them on their own terms" attitude. We have to listen to *their* story before we can tell them *our* story on the way to *the* story. Living on a mission field requires four huge shifts in how staff functions:

1. The shift from professional paid staff who direct volunteers in carrying out programs to paid servants who equip and coach unpaid servants to carry out most of the pastoral responsibilities. When this shift happens a church learns it can accomplish its goals with fewer paid staff.
2. The shift from using all paid staff to a combination of paid and unpaid servants to fill a role, or the use of unpaid servants as a

replacement for paid staff. When this shift occurs staff management becomes a key role for some key staff person.

3. The shift from seeing the needs of the congregation as the focus to seeing the penetration of the surrounding community as the focus. When this shift takes place the measurement of success changes.

4. The shift from a clear division between clergy and laity to more of an "it doesn't matter if you're ordained or not" attitude. When this shift takes place it frees up the church to develop the priesthood of believers.

So Why Have Staff at All?

Most people have a false understanding of why staff is needed. So let's be clear from the beginning: staff should *never* be hired to do ministry! That's right. The less ministry the staff does, the more people who are reached for Christ. And the more the kingdom grows and your church grows.

So what's the purpose of staff? Simply put, the role of staff is to "equip the saints for the work of ministry" (Eph. 4:12 ESV). Staff creates an environment in which leaders at every level are equipped and encouraged to replicate the DNA of the church by living out their spiritual gifts. God built the church on the premise that every Christian has a gift and a calling to share with the world. It's called the "priesthood of believers." The role of staff is to ensure this happens.

A Few Conversations Can Help

A couple of years ago we had the opportunity to pull together a group of thirty-four pastors from a variety of backgrounds to talk about why their churches weren't growing. Let's listen in on some of their conversations.

"I just don't understand why my church isn't growing," Sam said. "We were growing until we got to a little over a hundred in worship, and then we leveled off. We haven't grown any in the last year and I'm working harder than ever. Our volunteers are excellent, our fellowship is solid, and I'm preaching better than ever, but we can't seem to get over one hundred. What gives?"

"I don't understand either," Andy chimed in. "I hired the best worship leader we could afford and we rocketed to over three hundred in worship and then leveled off. Our worship is outstanding, but we can't seem to get over this barrier. I just don't understand."

"Well, I can go you one better," said Chuck. "The first five years we went from twenty to two thousand people in worship. Then we hit the wall and now we're on a plateau. Our staff is working harder than ever. We've added four new staff people. We can't figure out why we aren't growing."

Jim jumped in with his sad story. "I'm baffled too. We're stuck at two hundred in worship even after raising extra money to hire a full-time youth director. But that hasn't helped us grow one bit. I need help."

"I've got a different problem," said Toby. "We rapidly grew to four hundred and then began to decline. We're now around three hundred and I don't understand why, because we have the same worship, same programs, and same staff we had when we were at four hundred in worship. Everyone is working hard, but we've started declining and I don't have a clue."

Sarah finally unloaded. "We outgrew our space when we reached five hundred, so we built a new worship center and our attendance went to seven hundred overnight—but three years later we're down to about four hundred. I don't get it."

We began to ask some questions. We asked Sam what his plans were for hiring staff. His response was telling. "I haven't given that much thought. We're not a big church and don't have any money to staff. We've got to learn how to grow without paid staff."

Next we asked Andy, who was doing his children's ministry, to share his plans for hiring staff. "Volunteers," was his reply.

Then we asked Jim why he hired a youth director. He replied, "I've always heard that the youth are the future of the church."

We then turned to the megachurch pastor and asked him what plans he had for adding staff. Chuck's response was deadly. "I've already added four new staff the past three years. Surely you aren't saying I need to add more!"

At this point, we asked Sarah whether or not she built in additional staff to take care of the influx of people because of the new building. Her reply? "No. We could barely afford the building!"

Finally we asked Toby to describe his staff for us. His reply was all over the map. "We have two part-time program staff and one secretary. All of them are doing an excellent job. The only problem I have with the staff is I wish they had more relationships throughout the church."

So what's going on here?

After some conversation it was clear that these pastors had all committed a fatal mistake: they didn't understand the importance or the dynamics of staffing a church, much less staffing it for growth.

The thought of paid staff hadn't entered Sam's mind when he should have been looking for a worship leader. Andy was trying to take his church through the five hundred barrier with only two staff people. Chuck had allowed rapid growth to outgrow the staff's ability to form enough relationships to be able to identify and grow future leaders, so his church stopped growing. Jim hired a youth director when he should have hired a worship leader. Sarah allowed the church to build so it could expand, but she didn't think through the reality that more people always means more staff. Toby didn't understand that one staff person can only relate to a hundred people, and as a result he hadn't added any staff as they grew, and they receded back to the amount of people the staff could relate to.

So, here is our starting point: more than anything else, how a church staffs determines how many people a church can reach for Christ. A congregation's most valuable assets are the gifts, skills, and passion quotient of the paid staff. How a church staffs, and what it expects staff to accomplish, are two of the most important decisions church leaders ever make. A mistake here throws everything the congregation attempts out of balance.

The average church in the West doesn't grow beyond 125 in worship. Many reasons have been given for this inability to grow larger. Some blame it on the concept of the family

A congregation's most valuable assets are the gifts, skills, and passion quotient of the paid staff.

church, where the congregation prefers to know everyone rather than everyone in town knowing God. Others blame it on the dysfunctional nature inherent in small churches. Still others blame it on a lack of leadership from the lead pastor. While all of these obviously *could* play a part in the inability of small churches to grow, we don't think they are the primary reasons most churches stay below 125 in worship.

Our consulting experience and research have taught us the primary reason for the inability of churches to grow beyond 125 in worship is that no one in the church understands the importance and dynamics of staffing a church for growth. Most churches reach one hundred in worship without ever thinking about how they are going to staff the church. Instead of preparing the church for the addition of staff, the pastor just works harder and takes responsibility for more and more ministry, which eventually burns out the pastor and keeps the church from growing.

When a church is small one pastor can grow it without much help. We've seen pastors grow a church to four hundred in worship with almost no staff. We've also watched pastors like that crash and burn because they did not adequately staff the church. On the other hand, we've never seen a church grow beyond five hundred without the addition of paid staff.

As a church grows in size, the role of staff becomes more important.

In churches under 150 in worship nothing is more important than how the lead pastor recruits and equips unpaid servants. The key skill the pastor needs is learning how to hold these unpaid servants as accountable as paid staff would be. The biggest mistake made at this point is hiring (or recruiting) just anyone, whether or not they're qualified, and then failing to give them clear expectations.

In churches over 150 in worship nothing is more important than the lead pastor learning how to staff with paid people. The challenges the pastor faces here are that the people don't understand the need for paid staff, the pastor has difficulty relinquishing control of all ministry, the pastor hires someone to "do" ministry, or the pastor doesn't know how to manage people.

When a church reaches five hundred in worship, the primary challenge facing the lead pastor is the staffing issue. More time must be focused on staff as compared to the whole church. New skills are demanded of the pastor along with a willingness to allow others to receive the credit or the blame for their ministry. At this size it takes only one unaligned staff person to derail the entire progress of the church.

Our favorite way of describing the effects one ineffective staff person can have on the entire staff is to think of a stagecoach being pulled by eight horses in full gallop—and one of the horses decides to sit down. Can you imagine what would happen? That's the same thing that happens when all staff except one are hitting on all cylinders.

As churches grow beyond the one thousand mark staffing issues tend to be spread throughout the core staff, both paid and unpaid. It's not unusual for several paid staff to do the hiring and firing of those who work within their area of responsibility. Often this will be an office manager or business manager taking on the supervision of the office and maintenance people and/or an executive pastor supervising the pastoral/program staff. Or, in the case of multiple site congregations, the campus pastor taking responsibility for their campus's staff.

No matter what size it is, the number one reason a church plateaus or declines is because of staffing issues.

The Keystone of Staffing

A keystone is the central building block at the top of an arch that keeps the entire structure from collapsing. It is the anchor or central cohesive source that holds everything together. In the case of staffing an effective church, the keystone has four characteristics that apply to every staff member, no matter what position they have in the church.

1. Every staff person assists in equipping and sending people out into the mission field to be backyard missionaries. Everyone works for a single goal—the transformation of the individual, the community, and the world. Instead of seeing ministry taking place "at the church," they understand that ministry takes place "in the world."

2. The primary role of staff is to create a culture of transformation that produces disciples and leaders. Instead of seeing the

27

primary role of staff as taking care of people, they understand their primary role has become transforming people.

3. Staff functions as scouts and coaches rather than doers of ministry. Instead of being hired to *do* programs, staff members are hired to *be* scouts and coaches. They are always on the lookout for future leaders and are always coaching their current leaders to the next level. Like baseball scouts sent to the minor leagues, staff sees the church and surrounding community as a recruiting field, not to get people to sit on committees and do the bidding of the church, but to invite people into a growth process through which they find their place within the body of Christ. Everywhere staff members go, including Sunday morning and weekend services, they are scouting for future leaders. And when they find recruits, they understand their role is to coach them into a ministry that brings fulfillment to them and the body of Christ.

4. Each staff person does their share of generating both personal and numerical congregational growth. Once a church moves past three or four hundred in worship, explosive growth cannot rest solely on the shoulders of the lead pastor. Staff must assume more responsibility for growth. Each department in the church must have clearly defined growth goals that can be evaluated and for which they are held accountable throughout the year. Staff must feel the same pressure to grow their departments as the lead pastor feels for growing the church. Instead of a management mentality, all staff, including support staff, must have a growth mentality. Effective staff members identify and find ways around the growth barriers in their department.

These four paradigm shifts are fundamentally changing the game when it comes to staffing a church and being the Church.

Now we must turn our attention to how the congregation members function as backyard missionaries. Only when members begin functioning as backyard missionaries does viral evangelism become possible.

3

Staffing the Four Core Processes

Staffing an effective church is different than staffing an attractional church. The key difference is simple. In an effective church *every* staff person, including office and custodial personnel, has but one goal in mind: the transformation of individuals, the community, and the world. And yes, we can hear church members everywhere crying, "What about us?" We want to be clear. Effective churches take care of their own, but the care is at a different level. In Mark 1:30–31 Jesus healed Peter's mother-in-law. But notice what happens next:

> So he went to her, took her hand and helped her up. The fever left her and she began to wait on them.

Although she was healed, it wasn't so she could return to her once-a-week Sabbath worship service. She immediately began to serve. In an effective church every member is expected to be busy with kingdom work. Sure, the elderly are cared for, but taking care of them is not the primary thrust of the church, as shown in Acts 6.

Every effective church has four core processes that fuel its passion for transformation: (1) bring people to Christ and into the kingdom, (2) retain them, (3) disciple them, and (4) send them back out into society (see the diagram on p. 30).

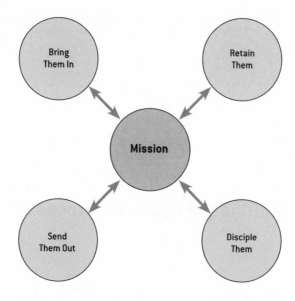

Each of these core processes has specific staffing needs, even in the smallest church. As we will show, the pastor alone may have the responsibility for all four processes, or it might be the pastor with either unpaid or paid staff. Regardless of the configuration, each process must be covered. Everything else the church does is insignificant. Yet we find few churches effectively staffing these four processes.

Most effective churches have multiple layers of staff. The first layer is the Peter, James, and John of the staff. These are the people who oversee the four core processes and meet with the lead pastor on a regular basis. The additional layers include the rest of the staff members who are ultimately responsible to the four core staff.

Introducing Fractals

There is a distinct difference between process and staff. Processes become to-dos and since one of the key points we're making is that leaders are not doers, we want to keep the lines of separation clear. Therefore we've named the staff positions for each core process as shown in the table below, as an example.

Process	Staff Position
Bring them in	Invite key leader
Retain them	Connect key leader
Disciple them	Apprentice key leader
Send them out	Send key leader

The staffing of the core processes structure can be seen graphically in the diagram below. This organizational structure is based on the biological phenomenon called fractaling. Fractals are naturally occurring repeated patterns such as those found in a tree leaf (the stem and veins in the leaf reflect the pattern of the trunk and branches). To understand this paradigm, consider the lead pastor. The lead pastor is ultimately responsible for the accomplishment of the church's mission: to make effective disciples of Jesus Christ. As we established earlier, mission fulfillment hinges on the effective accomplishment of the four core processes. In a church plant or very small church, the lead pastor is, for all practical purposes, solely responsible for all four processes. However, as the church grows, the core processes are handed off to gifted, called, and skilled staff members. This "handing off" process varies depending on context, but by the time a church reaches around five hundred in worship all four core processes should be in the hands of four paid staff members. In turn, the staff members "replicate" themselves based on the mission of their particular core process, just as the lead pastor has done.

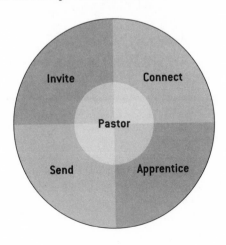

As we intimated earlier, the key leader for each core process is responsible for any and all processes and programs that contribute to the success of their core process. To best accomplish their mission, each key leader develops the processes necessary to accomplish their particular mission and raises up leaders who are called, gifted, and skilled. The diagram below illustrates an example of the fractalizations of the lead pastor and of each key leader (more on this in chapter 8). The strength of this model is that it is both flexible and scalable to any size church. The larger a church becomes, the more prolific the fractalization and the wider the reach of leadership as additional layers of fractals and leaders are added. The beauty of this model is that no one person ever "supervises" or is responsible for more than four leaders.

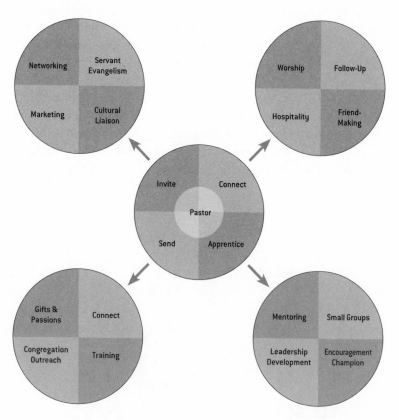

The Four Core Processes and Key Leaders

Since the configuration of additional layers varies from church to church based on context, we will focus primarily on the four staff positions overseeing the four core processes. We are not going to debate which process comes first—bringing in or sending out. Like the chicken and the egg, it's impossible to tell which comes first.

Each of these descriptions has two sections. There's an overview of the core process followed by a best-practices description for each of the key leaders. These descriptions reflect how a full-time staff member would focus their time and attention in order to ensure their core process was addressed.

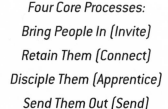

Four Core Processes:

Bring People In (Invite)

Retain Them (Connect)

Disciple Them (Apprentice)

Send Them Out (Send)

We realize that your church may not yet have five hundred or more in worship. No worries. Chapter 9 deals with how to adopt and adapt what you're going to learn in the next few chapters, plus how staff should be added as the church grows.

Now we turn our attention to the four core processes and how to staff them.

4

Process One

Bring People to Christ and into the Kingdom

The first step in growing an effective church is to gather people. The oversight of this process is in the hands of a person we call the Invite key leader (feel free to come up with your own title to fit your context). This person is responsible for doing whatever it takes to ensure there is a steady stream of new people coming to Christ and into the kingdom. You will notice the goal of this position is not necessarily to bring people into the local church. This distinction is crucial in understanding the effective church. An effective church is more focused on multiplying the kingdom than on the growth of the individual church (which ultimately leads to the growth of the local church).

A good example of this was the hiring of Curtis Sergeant by Saddleback church some years ago. Sergeant is known for his work with global house church movements and for being a catalytic leader in launching reproducing house churches. But rather than being hired to start a home group movement in the church, or even to start Saddleback satellite house churches, Sergeant was commissioned to begin house churches. Period. It was unimportant to Saddleback's leadership whether or not these house churches ever affiliated with Saddleback or whether or not they expanded the membership base of the mother church. Kingdom growth was their only concern.

Absolutely everything about growing a church depends on developing strategies for bringing people to Christ and the kingdom. When consulting with a church under five hundred in worship, we *always* recommend the lead pastor spend a considerable amount of time figuring out how to reach the community and then showing the congregation how to reach out and invite their networks. Note our use of the word *showing*. The lead pastor must be the chief practitioner of bringing people into the kingdom and into the local church. This is a key point that cannot be overemphasized: the congregation will only follow leaders who lead by example. How much time should the lead pastor spend on this core process? If the total average worship attendance is less than two hundred, we recommend the pastor spend 70 percent of their time connecting with the unchurched. If the total average worship attendance is between three and five hundred, we recommend the pastor spend 40 percent of their time connecting with the unchurched. When consulting with a larger church, we always ask if there is a staff member who spends at least twenty hours a week focusing on how *all* the staff can connect with the community—and if no one is, we recommend making that change.

Absolutely everything about growing a church depends on developing strategies for bringing people to Christ and the kingdom.

When we make the recommendation that the staff and the church reach out to the community, the most common question is, "How do I meet unchurched people?" When we hear this question we instantly know the staff is spending too much time at church. If finding ways to connect with your community is the focus of your every waking moment, you will *always* find a way to connect with unchurched people. However, here are some hints on how to connect with the unchurched.

35

Connecting with the Unchurched

Each community is different when it comes to reaching the unchurched. In every church we've pastored or consulted with, the key to the city has been different and required a different approach to reaching the unchurched people in the area. A cookie-cutter approach doesn't work. But there are some guidelines that will help:

Finding the key to the city is one of the most important tasks you'll ever do.

- In order to connect with the unchurched you must have four things: a heart for those far from God, knowledge of the community in which you serve, a personal story to tell, and a willingness to set aside significant and regular time to connect and establish relationships with the unchurched.

- Begin by setting aside regular time to brainstorm ways into the world of the unchurched in your community context. If you look for ways to connect long enough, you'll find the key to unlocking the door to the unchurched. Finding that key may take some time, but it is well worth the effort.

- Once you've found the key, set aside regular time to actually spend in the community. The smaller the church, the more time the pastor should spend in the community. As the church grows, the *oversight* of this responsibility should be handed off to the Invite key leader. However, no matter how big the church grows, one of the lead pastor's jobs is networking with the unchurched in the community. As the church grows, the amount of time and the selectivity with whom the pastor networks must change as well. As we suggested earlier, a pastor who doesn't regularly bring in new people ceases to be a model the congregation will follow.

- Mine the relationships new members have with the unchurched. New members are likely to have more relationships with unchurched people than long-term members. Ask them for an introduction to their unchurched friends. Better yet, encourage them to host a party, a dinner, or some other event for their networks and invite you to attend to meet their friends. And of course, get them to invite their networks to Christ and to your church.

- Although new members will likely have a larger unchurched network than most of your long-term members, undoubtedly your congregation has well-connected professionals who regularly rub shoulders with unchurched colleagues and clients. Teach these members to invite you to their social events such as golf tournaments, meet-and-greet parties, client appreciation receptions, and so on.

- Plan weekly practical deeds out in the community. It doesn't really matter what these events are as long as they do four things: bless the people you're helping, bless the city, bless those who are doing the practical deed, and provide visibility for your church. Notice that the church *must* get credit for being a blessing; do not do anything anonymously. Blessing the community is one of the most important ministries a church can undertake. In addition it is also one of the few ministries we've seen that often becomes intergenerational.

- Constantly ask two questions: "Who can we help who is hurting?" and "Who can we reach who is unreached?"

Best Practices of the Invite Key Leader

As we've said, the role of the Invite key leader is to ensure a steady stream of people are coming to Christ and into the kingdom. Although the position and title will vary from church to church depending on the context, there are some specific best practices for the position. This person:

- **Models spirituality.** The most important characteristic of every member, and especially of every staff member, is their conspicuous model of faith. In today's culture it matters little what you say. Words have never been so cheap. Effective disciples of Jesus Christ model their faith wherever they go and in everything they do.

- **Champions inviting.** The Invite key leader lives, breathes, and talks invite. Indeed, this is the lens through which they measure everything the church is doing. They are always asking, "How will this invite those outside the faith (and the church) into a meaningful relationship with an effective, faithful disciple of Jesus Christ?" They don't just champion inviting people to church; theirs is a kingdom worldview. They realize that today's unchurched people come to faith almost exclusively because of a friendship with an authentic disciple of Jesus.

- **Ensures inviting is a staff priority.** The one drawback of having an invite champion is the tendency for complacency by the rest of the staff and the congregation—after all, doesn't so-and-so have that covered? But inviting is a fundamental responsibility for *every* staff member of the church and the Invite key leader is the squeaky wheel that constantly reminds them. In addition, they help the staff create and/or maintain an invite focus when planning events, programs, and ministries. Ultimately, every church position description should include a specific, measurable goal of how many unchurched folks must become active in the church through the personal invitation of each staff member every year.

- **Creates and maintains an inviting culture.** Nothing grows a church faster than rabid (in a good way) members who can't help but invite their Friends, Relatives, Acquaintances, Neighbors, Co-workers, and Everyone else (yes, it spells France). To that end, the Invite key leader does everything possible to make it easy for the church to invite. From the creation of hand-offs[1] for every event including worship to providing "How to Invite" training classes, videos, webinars, blog posts, articles, etc., the Invite key leader does whatever it takes to incite an inviting pandemic.

- **Manages church marketing.** The best definition we've seen for the word *marketing* is this: "To make friends." Once upon a time, a church could take out a weekly ad in the newspaper and, in some locales, legitimately believe that this was effective marketing. Today, most churches can ill-afford mass marketing for the simple reason that the return on their investment is so low. Therefore, the Invite key leader is market savvy and maximizes every opportunity. They overhaul the church newsletter into a powerful invite tool, funnel significant funds to the church's web presence, take control of the church's message sign so that it's a marketing tool rather than an expensive billboard for clever (but pointless) fortune cookie aphorisms, and generate community buzz by creating marketing campaigns rather than relying on piecemeal advertising efforts. For maximum effectiveness, we recommend spending at least 10 percent of the church's annual budget on marketing efforts.

Process one: bring people to Christ or the church. How much time do you or a staff person spend each week connecting with the unchurched?

- **Creates fishing pools.**[2] These are social events where both members and nonmembers come together. It has been well established that building relationships is the first step toward bringing people to Christ and the kingdom. Some examples might be a golf tournament or a block party for the neighborhood. An excellent book to help you in this area is *Heartbeat* by Charles Arn.[3]

- **Interprets culture.** One of the realities of well-churched people is that they quickly lose touch with the fast-changing "real world." Technology isn't the only thing traveling in the ludicrous speed lane. Idioms, slang, terminology, catch-phrases, and even new words are created and morph faster than someone can update their status on ~~MySpace~~ ~~Friendster~~ ~~Bebo~~ ~~Twitter~~ Facebook. . . . The Invite key leader not only keeps up with the changing culture through the eyes and hearts of the local community, they interpret that culture to the staff to ensure relevance in communication as well as in event, program, ministry, and mission planning. In addition they interpret culture for the lead pastor to ensure relevant sermon preparation and delivery.

- **Develops invitation campaigns.** The Invite key leader champions, plans, and implements "Bring a Friend"–type campaigns where the goal is to train members to invite their networks and double the number of first-time visitors. We recommend the "I Love My Church" campaign.[4]

Now that we have the first process under our belt, let's examine process two: retaining people long enough to disciple them. It should be obvious that unless first-time guests return, it becomes more difficult to disciple them.

5

Process Two

Retain People Long Enough to Disciple Them

You may think bringing people to your church is difficult, but retaining them is even more difficult. The vast majority of people who visit a church don't return, and those who do rarely remain long enough to be discipled, let alone developed into spiritual leaders. Getting people connected is too often left to chance in a church. A first-time guest with little or no church experience typically goes through a three-step connecting process.

1. They connect with the church's ethos. In general, they attend a worship service where the music, message, and culture resonate with them. They are somehow moved, touched, inspired, or simply have a good enough time that they're willing to return.
2. They connect with someone in the church. They make a friend or two and begin spending time with them. In return, these friends become mentors whose faith rubs off on the "guest."
3. They connect with God. How *our* spirit connects with *the* Spirit is shrouded in mystery. What we do understand is that in a church context the connection generally happens in one

of three ways: via group discipleship, mentoring, or worship. The key to remember is that the connection of spirit to Spirit doesn't happen overnight. Indeed, recent evidence suggests it typically takes around three years from first connection with a church ethos and/or a mentor-friend to an intentional profession of faith.

This section is about how to create a connecting culture so that your first-time guests become returning guests and ultimately become faithful disciples of Jesus Christ. Of course, if they happen to join your church, so much the better!

We've found four things cause people to stick around long enough to be discipled:

- Welcoming hospitality that helps them feel accepted and appreciated
- Worship that connects with their spirit
- Consistent follow-up
- Making six or seven good friends within the first ninety days

Let's take a closer look at these four retention pieces.

Welcoming Hospitality

Every church we've ever consulted with has assured us they're one of the friendliest churches in town. But here's a reality check: to someone who's never darkened the doors of a church building, there really is no such thing as a *friendly* church. It takes a lot of courage to go to church for the first time. At best, church is perceived as a foreign culture with peculiar values, practices, and rites. At worst, church is perceived as hostile territory filled with judgmental hypocrites just waiting to point their fingers and look down their noses.

In its simplest form, hospitality is helping guests feel both welcome and "at home." Welcoming hospitality does two things. First, it removes any barriers that may stand between a guest and a connection. Second, it makes it possible for the guest to objectively hear the gospel.

A whole book could be written on effective church hospitality (in fact, I [BTB] am in the midst of writing one); however, we want to highlight some key hospitality issues that we find missing or misapplied in many, if not most, churches.

One, hospitality should begin in the parking lot. Study after study has shown that guests form their first impressions within the first few minutes, and the clock starts ticking before the guest gets parked. If you don't have a parking lot hospitality team, form one *this week* and charge them with at least three tasks: (1) deploy visible parking attendants to help guests and members find parking spots, (2) greet guests and members in the parking lot and help them make their way into the church building, and (3) direct traffic as guests and members arrive and leave—and thank folks for coming.

Two, exterior directional signs should be plentiful, easily seen, and well lit. In every parking lot, including the ones that "only members use," there should be signage that points the way to the worship center and to childcare (if located separately from the worship center). In addition, every single door should be labeled, including doors that "everyone knows aren't used." If a door is kept locked, a sign saying so should be visible from a distance so a guest doesn't have to wend their way to it only to discover it's not an entrance.

Three, greeters take their posts *outside* of their doors at least twenty minutes before a worship service or event and remain there at least fifteen minutes after the opening. Your greeters should also take their posts again five minutes before the service ends so they can hold doors, thank folks for coming, and invite folks to return next week. Recruit your friendliest, smiley, most positive, guest-aware people for your front doors. If you recruit people who do this naturally (that is, they're called to it), you won't have any problems getting them to "own" their posts . . . in fact, it may even be difficult to get them to take a break! On the flip side, if you have any grumpy greeters you're better off retiring them immediately, even if this might cause some heartache. You don't get a second chance to make a good first impression.

Four, once a guest gets inside, they'll be looking for two or three things. If they have children, they may want to find childcare. If they're seriously looking for a church, they may look for a prominent and friendly information center. But the number one thing they'll be looking for is your restrooms. We know by experience, research, and hundreds of interviews that the most important room in a church is the restroom. Your restrooms should be modern, with gender sensitive décor and scents, and include a hand sanitizer dispenser and diaper changing table in both the women's *and* men's restrooms. Of course, having great restrooms is totally pointless if your guests can't find them. Interior signage is critical. Here's the rule of thumb: no matter where you stand in your church building, you should be able to see a sign that points you to (1) the worship center, (2) the nearest restroom, and (3) the nursery. Signs should be perpendicular to the wall so they can be seen without having to walk up to each door to find out whether it's the boys' room, a Sunday school classroom, or the furnace room.

Five, build a prominent, easy to find, well-staffed, and well-stocked information center . . . and do not call it the visitor booth or welcome center. Information centers have more than just first-time guest packets. Most first-time guests would rather not be publicly identified in any way and they know they're "marked" if they stop by a visitor or welcome booth. The information center should be "staffed" by two of your sharpest cookies who are some of the warmest and friendliest folks in the church and are familiar with virtually every ministry the church offers; the key points of the church's history; and the church's DNA, including its mission, core values, vision, and key beliefs. Their key job is to be at the booth before and after services (same schedule as the greeters) and to keep an eye out for those who are clearly out of their element and need a friendly face to assist them.

Six, your nursery must meet the criteria of the five S's. It should be **Staffed** by at least two unrelated adults who have had thorough background checks (youth are not adequate nursery workers unless they are a third or fourth pair of hands). It should be a **Safe** environment with no way for a child to be hurt. Your nursery should be visibly **Sanitary** with prominent wall-mounted hand sanitizer dispensers near the changing table, in the restroom, and by the nursery door. All hard surfaces should be sanitized after each use (not just at the end of the service) and bedding should be changed after each use as well. **Security** is a huge issue in the church today. The nursery, and the whole children's wing for that matter, should have restricted access so that a noncustodial parent (or anyone else) can't easily get to the children. We find that small churches often minimize these concerns, but we want to ask: How's that working for you? Are young families visiting and staying? You'd be sadly surprised how many families are affected by custodial issues. A word to the wise: don't blow this off. And finally, your nursery (and all of your child-space) should **Sizzle**. Today's parents go out of their way to provide learning environments for their children, beginning at the newborn stage. The adage, "Momma decides where the family will go to church, and the kids decide if they'll return" is more true today than ever.

Seven, train and deploy ushers, lobby hosts, and worship center hosts to carry hospitality to the next level. Ushers should ush.[1] Lobby hosts should look for the lost and point them in the right direction. Worship center hosts should greet and chat with folks they don't know and those they don't know well.

Your goal for worship is to create a safe place to hear a dangerous gospel; not a dangerous place to hear a safe gospel.

Eight, "You're a host, not a guest." Every member of the congregation needs to personalize this phrase and internalize it so they understand why they have to move to the center of the pew when it's crowded or when an usher asks them to. It's every member's responsibility to greet and have conversations with those they don't know or don't know well.

Before you invite anyone to your church for any event, make sure your hospitality is second to none.

Worship That Connects People to God

Although your hospitality may be above reproach, if the worship doesn't resonate with your guests' spirits they're not going to hang around long.

Worship is the bread and butter of any church. As goes the worship service, so goes the church. The key to creating a worship service that connects with a guest's spirit is to design the worship service with them in mind. We're not talking about dumbing down your theology or pandering to the whims of culture. The gospel message is unchanging, but *effective presentation* must be, and always has been, culturally relevant. If your worship doesn't speak the language of your guests, they'll be unable to hear the gospel.

Of course language is about the words you try to communicate with, but it includes so much more. Today's culture speaks through word choice, music, style, body language, and technology. A worship service that says "Everyone is welcome" but includes church jargon and traditional hymnody performed on traditional instruments really communicates "Only those with a churched background are welcome." A worship service where a guest in gothic attire and multiple piercings experiences sidelong glances, women shifting their purses, and being given a wide berth communicates "Only those who look (and likely act) like we do are welcome." And a worship service where the sole teaching style is auditory communicates "Only those born before the MTV generation are welcome."

Please hear us clearly: we're not suggesting upending your traditional worship service. Indeed, we *never* suggest transitioning a well-done classic worship service into anything other than an even more effective and well-done classic worship service. But we *do* advocate being honest about whose spirit will resonate with the service or services you have. A traditional service should be an excellent service that touches the heartstrings of those who are moved by that style. The same is true with any other service you might host: it should communicate effectively and resonate with those you're intending to reach. Don't expect the average eighty-year-old lifelong church member to resonate with an R&B service—some might, but most won't. And don't expect a never-churched under-thirty-year-old to resonate with even an excellent classic worship service—again, some might, but most won't.

Therefore, before you spend money on anything else, you must make sure your worship communicates the gospel effectively. Remember, as goes worship so goes the church; therefore, every aspect of your worship service must be top-notch, especially your worship staff. With that in mind, your first hire should *always* be a worship leader (we'll expound on this more later).

We've found there are several general dos and don'ts when it comes to providing a worship experience that connects people to God.

Worship Don'ts

- Never begin with announcements. Instead, begin a traditional service with the best choir anthem of the day and an indigenous service with either the best chorus or chorus set. *Never* begin by welcoming people verbally—always open with music or a video.

Your first hire should always be a worship leader.

- Never ask visitors to identify themselves during worship. Instead use some form of registration. They will let you know when they are ready to be known. The fastest way to run off unchurched people is to ask them to identify themselves in worship.

- Never mention a long list of ill people during a prayer time or allow people from the congregation to mention someone in need of prayer. Just consider how long the list would be if your church were twice its size. In addition, HIPAA laws prohibit health-related announcements without written authorization. It is better to nix it from the beginning than to spend the time trying to get permissions.

- Never leave the congregation wondering what to do with your sermon's message. Always conclude with a "What now?"

- In a traditional service never use such elements as the Gloria Patri or the Lord's Prayer without including the full text. Never expect guests to look it up in the book. The congregation will be finished reciting by the time they find it. Remember, most of the country today has little or no Christian memory.

- Never expect first-time guests to put money in the offering plate. Instead ask them to put the prayer or registration card in the plate instead of money, since they are your guests.

- In a traditional service, never have a long organ prelude. Also, limit the length of the offertory instrumental to time needed for the offering rather than the number of notes on the sheet music.

47

And don't allow a classically trained musician to convince you otherwise.

- Never mix contemporary and traditional elements unless you launched the services that way in the first place. All it does is leave everyone unfulfilled.

Worship Dos (For All Services)

- Make sure the service is planned and presented with the unchurched in mind.
- Always remember that music is as important as the sermon.
- Avoid dead spots. A dead spot is when nothing happens for five seconds or more unless it is a planned meditation. One of the most common dead times in a traditional service is waiting for the choir to get ready to sing. In a contemporary service the most common dead time is between music pieces.[2]
- In a traditional service the adult choir should sing every Sunday, even when a youth or children's choir also sings.
- Evaluate your worship service to discover where it isn't yet up to par. That's where you need to spend your time, energy, and money before moving on to something else. In fact, don't even invite people to visit until your worship service is between good and excellent. The first impression rule applies here. If the worship experience is lacking, you can't retain guests.

Best Practices of the Worship Pastor/Leader

A worship leader is different from a choir director.

We've seldom seen a thriving church without an excellent worship leader. This person is more than a choir director. The role of this person isn't just to direct a choir or lead a band. The role of the worship leader is to prepare those on stage to represent God so fully that the congregation connects with God.

No matter whether your worship is traditional or contemporary, there are some things every worship leader should do. Let's take a look at some of them.

- Maintain a growing relationship with Jesus Christ. We can't give what we don't have, so a fresh and strong spiritual life is essential to leading worship. We've been in some churches where the choir director wouldn't go to church if they weren't being paid to direct the choir.

- Spend time developing relationships with non-Christians both to advance the kingdom as well as to understand the community well enough to design worship to connect with it. This is "Job One" of *every* staff person. Remember, you never do anything without the unchurched in mind.

- Build the necessary teams to produce worship that brings people into the presence of God. A worship leader isn't hired to be a performer (although they could be). Gathering musicians and taking them deeper into their faith and ability to lead worship is this person's main task.

- Plan the corporate worship services in consultation with the lead pastor.

- Coordinate the theme of the day with the musical and technical aspects of the service.

- Oversee song and choral selection, media preparation and presentation, sound and lighting enhancements, and coordination of all instrumentalists, vocalists, and dramatists.

- Serve as lead worshiper in all worship services.

- Direct all weekly activities and rehearsals necessary to facilitate worship in services.

- Provide pastoral care for the worship teams and choirs.

- Oversee the worship department budget, organization, and volunteers.

- Be a scout for future musicians so there is always a replacement in mind or another team for a new service or site.

As you can see, the role of a worship leader is far different from that of a typical choir director. The typical choir director merely gets a choir ready to perform, whereas a worship leader choreographs the service, rehearses the band, and shepherds those in the music ministry.

Consistent Follow-Up

It takes a good bit of courage for someone to visit a new church, even if they come as an invited guest of a close friend. Great hospitality will help them feel more at home. Great worship will resonate within their spirit. But even a good first impression doesn't mean they'll return a second time. However, you can significantly increase the odds of a second visit by engaging an effective follow-up process.

The converse is true as well. If a church doesn't respond to a first-time guest within twenty-four hours, the odds are 75 percent they *won't* return.

Keep in mind there is no one way to respond to first-time guests. In some parts of the country a drop-in visit works well; in other parts of the country a drop-in visit could at best be unwanted and at worst it might be dangerous. But no matter what steps you take, it's important that a staff person makes personal contact within twenty-four hours. In churches with fewer than five hundred in worship the lead pastor should make these contacts. In larger churches the Connect key leader is responsible for ensuring these contacts are made.

I (BE) was working in a church recently that averaged eight hundred in worship and had eighteen first-time families attend worship on an average week. This is *easily* enough first-time guests to rocket a church through the one thousand barrier. Nonetheless, the church was declining. When I asked how they followed up on those first-timers, they replied, "We send them a letter." "Then what?" I asked. They looked at me as if I was crazy to even ask the question. They had no idea what effective follow-up looked like.

If you are part of a megachurch you may feel as if this section doesn't apply to you, because you have so many visitors and it appears impossible to follow our suggestions. But you need to know this: the main problem we've seen in megachurches is they have a huge back door and lose more people than they retain. We're convinced that one key reason for this is that they use size as an excuse to not make a *personal* connection with each first-time guest who signs in. A consistent follow-up is as important for the megachurch as for any other size church.

Effective follow-up is based on the amount of contact information a guest provides and cultural context.[3] We'll say more about context later, but in a nutshell the lead pastor (or the Connect key leader if average worship exceeds five hundred) must make personal contact with every guest within twenty-four hours. If you have an address, stop by their house and follow that with a handwritten note on personal stationery—not a form letter with a signature. If you only have a phone number, call them. If you only have an email address, send them a personal email that includes an invitation to next week's worship and give them your sermon topic.

Here are the steps and the details for effectively responding to first-timers. Remember, everything about discipleship begins here. Failure to respond in a timely and relevant manner results in fewer returnees.

Step One: The Two-Minute Visit

The afternoon of the visit, the lead pastor or a team of servants take a gift to the first-time guests (if this won't work in your area, see Step One Fallback). This is a front door, porch-side visit that includes thanking the guest for visiting, presenting them with a gift, and inviting them to return. The visit should take no more than two minutes and the temptation to accept an invitation to come inside should be politely declined. (If you have more contact information than an address, the pastor or paid staff person should *also* call, write, or email within twenty-four hours.)

The drop-off gift should have staying power and create a lasting impression. Cakes and cookies are gone in a day or two, so it's best not to use them. The gift needs to be something that will linger, such as a coffee mug, a potted plant, a CD, and so forth. Here are some examples.

- One church takes each guest a small potted ivy with a note saying, "We hope you will nourish your spiritual life just like you need to water this plant daily." They also include the name of a contact person at the church.
- Another church invites guests to visit the information center after the service to receive a small gift bag that includes a

church-branded honey pot and a small jar of honey provided by a parishioner. Later that afternoon the lead pastor drops off a freshly baked loaf of bread to go with the honey as well as information about the church.

- Many churches give a mug with the name and mission statement of the church printed on it. Some stuff the mug with goodies such as Starbucks Via coffee packs, candies, or pens.

- Still others deliver a bag or basket of goodies including a mug, a CD or DVD introducing them to the church, and a flier about new member orientation.

- The best impression-making response we've ever seen was the delivery of a FedEx package Monday or Tuesday afternoon to the guest family. The box included a VeggieTales DVD for the children, a photograph of each child having fun in the church's children's space, a CD with a welcome from the pastor and an introduction to their adult ministries, a 25 percent discount to the church bookstore, an invitation to the next pastor's gathering, a gas gift card, and an assortment of other items including an easy-to-read Bible. Not only can the church be sure that every FedEx package is opened, but that their welcome package makes an exceptional impression. Indeed, it is such a "wow" experience their guests tell their friends, who tell their friends, thus making the church's guest-friendly reputation into the stuff of legend.

No matter what type of response you choose, make sure you do as much as you can and do it consistently. A gift basket with a variety of helpful items is better than just one item. The younger the family, the more likely they will respond to a well-done CD or DVD introducing them to the church, its leaders, and its ministries. Remember, a welcome gift that totally wows your guests means that even if they don't return, they'll tell their network of friends, family, and associates. A word to the wise: don't scrimp on the welcome gift.

Step One Fallback: Appointment Setting

For churches located where drop-in visits are impractical or unwanted, you may need to fall back to appointment setting.[4] Within twenty-four hours, every guest who signs in should be called. Again, it is best if the lead pastor makes these calls. The outcome of this contact will vary based on the response by the visitor. Ultimately, the goal is to get an appointment for a home or office visit. An in-person visit is the most effective way to ensure a guest's return. However, some won't be open to a personal visit. Others may be more open to an email. Still others may not be open to any further contact with the church. However, we do know this: if you set up an in-home or office appointment the odds of the guest returning to the church greatly increase.

When you make the call, take note of the guest's receptivity using a scale similar to this one:

1	No future contact other than mailing
3–5	Email contact
6–8	Personal and/or email
9–10	The more personal the contact, the better

This call record should be passed along to whoever is responsible for the next follow-up steps.

Step Two: Thank-You Note

One of the biggest mistakes many churches make in guest follow-up is that they send impersonal, generic form letters. Sure, the lead pastor may actually sign the letter, but you can be certain no one is going to be impressed by it. Remember, making a lasting impression is the key to effective follow-up.

Whether or not the lead pastor has made a home visit, a phone call, or both in step one, the next step is a handwritten, personalized thank-you note. This note should be written on a nice notecard or stationery. It should be concise and include a thank-you for attending, some personal words if possible, an invitation to the upcoming worship service with mention of the sermon title, and the offer to be of service or to answer any questions if needed. This note should be in the mail no later than Monday afternoon.

Of course, if you don't have a mailing address, but you do have an email address, respond similarly with a personal email.

Step Three: Data Management

Each guest should be placed into a database, along with any particulars about the family such as receptivity, family members, hobbies, interests, and so forth. Then this family or individual should be tracked over the next ninety days to see if they return and if they are plugging into any church ministries. Someone on staff should be responsible for the follow-up from this point on. If the family has children, the staff person in charge of children should be given their names to make contact either by email, mail, phone, or all three depending on the receptivity level of the family. The Connect key leader should keep the focus on the first-time guests at each staff meeting.

Step Four: Mailings

An email and/or mailing designed specifically for first-time guests should be sent later in the week. This must not take the place of the thank-you note in step two. This should be a professional-looking brochure or flier that introduces guests to the key ministries of the church as well as to the staff. The piece should include more graphics than words and be kept to no more than one page front and back. Color is expected.

In addition, put guests on your newsletter mailing list (if you have one). You'll want to be sure your newsletter is guest-friendly and not filled with insider information that is irrelevant to nonmembers.

Step Five: Group Connections

If your church has an active small group ministry, give the guest's name and contact information to a small group that's based around the guest's interests, family structure, or geographic location, or utilizes an established friendship with a small group leader or person in a small group. If your church has a strong Sunday school program, give the guest's information to the Sunday school class (or classes, in the case of families with children) that best fits. Either the leader or someone from the class should contact the family or individual and extend an invitation. This can be done by phone, email, or postcard depending on the receptivity level and available contact information. The Connect key leader should follow up to ensure the small group leader or Sunday school leader made the contact and invitation.

Step Six: Connection Tracking

During the next three months each guest's connectivity with the congregation should be closely monitored by the Connect key leader. Never give oversight of this responsibility to a volunteer. During these three months, depending on the guest's level of involvement, the Connect key leader may want to contact them either at church or at home to see what questions they have, how well they're connecting with their small group, if they are ready to take on some ministry responsibility, and if they need more information about Christ or joining the church. However, people should not be made to feel they have to become members in order to participate in or lead a ministry (the further we go into the twenty-first century, the less importance will be given to membership and more importance to participation). We have found that the faster a first-time guest is involved in a ministry, the more likely they are to stick with you long enough to be discipled.

During these three months it is imperative that the first-time guest become friends with at least five to seven people in the church. Without making these connections, the odds are the family or individual will drop out in eighteen to twenty-four months. This is why participation beyond worship is crucial.

Step Seven: Long-Term Follow-Up

If the first-time guest hasn't returned in three months, take them off your regular database and put them in an inactive database (they may return later and you will want to keep what information you already have). However, we recommend leaving them on your newsletter mailing list for at least one year unless they specifically ask to be removed. If your follow-up made a significant and positive impression, some event or sermon series may trigger their interest enough to return.

Making New Friends

Although your guests may be wowed by your hospitality, resonate with your worship service, and are impressed by your follow-up, retaining them long enough to disciple them will require their making a few good friends within the first three months. If they don't, it is unlikely they will be with you two years later.

In virtually every effective church we've worked with, we've found that small group ministry is the most effective incubation system for retaining people. Small groups are also especially effective at discipleship and leadership development. Everyone needs a place where someone knows more than just their name. Small groups help people build lasting friendships faster and more successfully than Facebook and speed dating combined. Most effective small groups meet in homes on a regular basis to share life, develop leaders, fellowship around the Scriptures, and participate in a ministry focused on transforming the community. The goal of most effective small groups that retain people is leadership development, behavior modification, and the multiplication of groups.

The difference between small groups and either missional communities or house churches is that small groups are attached to a local church.[5] Small groups may look and even act like missional communities or house churches, but they are the backbone of a local congregation.

Best Practices of the Small Group Ministry Leader

For a small group ministry to be truly effective, it requires someone who's responsible for training and managing the groups. We've never seen a full-blown small group ministry that includes more than 50 percent of the church without at least a half-time paid small group ministry leader. Every effective small group ministry leader we've encountered does at least the following:

- Designs and implements a system that results in at least 60 to 70 percent of the church (both members and nonmembers) in small groups that raise up new leaders, share life together, hold each other accountable, share the Scriptures, participate in a community ministry, and multiply into more small groups even if only one person leaves the group to begin another group.

- Develops monthly and/or quarterly opportunities for new people to be easily assimilated into a small group.[6]
- Develops and implements monthly, bimonthly, or quarterly training for all small group leaders.
- Touches base each week with the volunteer or paid staff who coaches small group leadership clusters (ten to fifteen small group leaders).
- If a variety of curriculum is used, oversees the selection of curriculum available to the small groups. However, we're finding that one of the best ways to provide good, inexpensive curriculum is for the small groups to base their discussions around the previous week's sermon. Discussing the sermon greatly reduces the leader's preparation time, making it easier to raise up leaders for small groups. You can read more about this model in Larry Osborne's book *Sticky Church*.[7]

Best Practices of the Connect Key Leader

The Connect key leader is ultimately responsible for all the processes, programs, and practices of the Retain Them core process. This includes hospitality, worship, follow-up, and any other activity that facilitates the integration/assimilation of a guest into the congregation and then into service as a fully functioning follower of Jesus Christ. It isn't an overstatement to say that the Connect key leader has oversight for every process that moves a guest from visitor to disciple and then sends them back into the community as a backyard missionary.

Therefore, the Connect key leader accomplishes the following:

- Coordinates connecting ministries, programs, and processes with the Invite, Apprentice, and Send key leaders.
- Ensures the congregational hospitality is exceptionally welcoming.
- Ensures every worship service not only has guests in mind, but has been planned and executed to resonate with their spirits.
- Sets up an integration/assimilation system that moves people from the marketplace to participation in the church and then back out into the marketplace. The specifics of how this is achieved doesn't

matter as long as its results grow the kingdom.

- Responds within twenty-four hours to every first-time visitor who signs in, and ensures the follow-up procedures are both practiced and effective.

- Tracks every guest from their first visit through their deployment into mission.

- Oversees small group and/or Sunday school programming. It's imperative that a new adult small group or Sunday school class is started periodically. In churches under two hundred in worship, a new group or class should be started at least every quarter. In larger churches, start a new group or class at least monthly.

Process two: retain them. What kind of bonding agent do you have at your church to retain people?

We still have two core processes to discuss, so let's get to them.

6

Process Three

Disciple Those Who Return

Missionaries know the quickest way to disciple a person is to involve them in hands-on ministry. It doesn't matter if they are a Christian or not—just get them involved in helping others and watch the transformation take place.

In order to make disciples, most church leaders have to make a radical paradigm shift, essentially from believing their primary job is to provide in-house programs or ministries to understanding that their primary job is to apprentice and equip leaders to live out the Christian life among their everyday neighbors and networks.

Many people confuse discipleship with classroom teaching. But you can't "teach" a prepackaged curriculum that will make a disciple. The truth is, *you* are the curriculum. Every Christian's role is to hang out with people and let them see Jesus in them. If you look closely at what Jesus did, you'll find he used the following formula:

1. I do; you watch; we'll talk.
2. You do; I watch; we'll talk.
3. You do; someone else watches; you'll talk.

Process three: apprentice them so they become Christlike. How much time do you devote to discipling one-on-one? How much of your staff meetings do you devote to discipling staff members?

Many readers will recognize the medical model in Jesus's teaching plan: see one; do one; teach one. If you take this formula seriously, you'll realize that discipleship is more on-the-job-training with you as the main curriculum than it is a classroom data-dump. You should also realize this is the primary responsibility of all Christians. And if you take a deep breath, you'll realize discipleship is synonymous with leadership development. Discipleship and leadership multiplication is one of the primary reasons the effective church exists. This concept is so important we've devoted chapters 8 and 9 to discipleship and leadership development.

Effective disciples don't live the Jerusalem church model. Instead they emulate the Antioch church paradigm—they can't wait to get out and make a difference in their neighborhood, their community, and to the ends of the earth. The next chapter will prepare you for helping disciples to "Go!"

7

Process Four

Send Them Back Out into the World

Unlike most attractional churches that recruit people to work on committees or ministries within the church building, effective churches commission most of their leaders and congregation to work on ministries focused outside the church building. Putting people on a committee is the fastest way to lose them, whereas inviting them to work in a meaningful ministry outside the church is the quickest way to disciple them. In addition, when you send them into the community to serve, they don't lose their relationships with unchurched people.

We're continually guided by Jesus's words to his disciples in John 4:35, "I tell you, open your eyes and look at the fields! They are ripe for harvest." We live right in the middle of the world's biggest mission field; we don't have to go into all the world—the world is all around us. A missional church recognizes this reality and effectively prepares and sends its members back into that mission field: our own backyards. We call those faithful disciples backyard missionaries. Today many churches are sending out backyard missionaries into their city, but we want to mention three legendary examples.

Backyard Missionaries

One of the very first churches to tap into this idea of the backyard missionary was The Vineyard Community Church of Cincinnati, Ohio. Several years ago, while working with them in a pastoral leadership transition, I (BE) had firsthand experience with the outreach they called "Random Acts of Kindness." One Saturday I witnessed over a hundred people gather to go into the community to clean toilets for businesses, give water away at Wal-Mart, clean cigarette butts from the exit ramps on the freeway, and take on an assortment of other kind acts.[1]

The Healing Place in Baton Rouge, Louisiana, is another fine example. Every day dozens of servants are blessing the city by mowing and cleaning yards, hosting block parties, painting houses, cleaning schools in the inner city, passing out chewing gum to students on LSU's campus, giving out cold drinks to drivers stuck in rush hour traffic on hot summer afternoons, reaching out to several assisted living facilities and nursing homes in the community, distributing food and gifts to the Baton Rouge area, as well as doing similar deeds from their other campuses all over the world. They call these actions "Servolution." The leaders insist that Servolution is a culture, not a program. Serving is who the people of the Healing Place are.

Our third example is the Dream Center in Los Angeles, California. I (BE) first ran into their pastor, Matthew Barnett, while writing a book with Dave Travis of Leadership Network.[2] Every day thousands of dollars of food and medical supplies are carried into the city by hundreds of servants from the Dream Center.

We believe, at least at this point in time, that churches like these across the country do more good and reach more people than all the "missional communities" combined. We also believe the reason local churches are only reaching 35 percent of the US population is because they are not sending out backyard missionaries. Instead they're stuck in the "Y'all come" paradigm of the Jerusalem church. We're convinced that as more local churches send people into their communities to be a blessing, the percentage of people reached by the local church will grow.

So let's take a few moments for an exercise. List all your programs and ministries that keep people occupied within your church. Then list the ministries that intentionally send your people outside the church. Go ahead. Take the time to make the two lists before moving on.

How did you come out?

Is the first list longer than the second list? If so, is it any wonder that after fewer than three years of participating in your church your new members no longer have any unchurched friends? We hope you get the picture. If your goal is to get new people "involved in the church," they'll quickly lose

What does your church do to send people back out into the world to transform it, transform them, and bring more people into the church and the kingdom?

connection with most of the unchurched world. So equip them to use their gifts among their natural relationships. Although it seems counterintuitive, getting your members (and guests) to serve the church is a guaranteed way to shrink the church.

Best Practices of the Send Key Leader

The responsibility of the Send key leader is to get as many people as possible out into the community and world doing hands-on ministry each week. It doesn't matter what these community or world ministries are as long as they are blessing both the people who are serving and those who are being served, as well as blessing the city and increasing the visibility of the church.[3] With that in mind, here are the Send key leader's best practices:

- Get to know their community and city well enough to:
    1. Scope out various community and city needs.
    2. Find existing agencies and networks that are meeting community and city needs.
    3. Bless the community and city by plugging servants into these existing agencies and networks.

4. Bless the community and city by facilitating the creation of ministries that provide for needs unmet by existing agencies and networks.

- Organize and oversee numerous weekly ministries in the community as well as several world ministries each year.
- Recruit and train leaders for all of the above.

Effective Antioch-type churches rely less on seminary-trained staff and more on home-grown leaders. Therefore, leadership multiplication becomes a primary function of every effective church. So we turn now to a discussion on how to multiply your leadership base, which returns us to a discussion of discipling and apprenticing new leaders.

Process four: send them back out to invite their networks. Do you commission more people to go out into the community to serve than you nominate to offices in the church?

8

Leadership Multiplication

We are living in an era when the demand for leadership far outstrips the supply in every arena, including pastors and staff. The pool is at an all-time low, especially among mainline denominations. So we're not surprised when we're constantly asked what it takes to apprentice more mature disciples.

But the real problem arises when people ask us their follow-up question: "Where do we find the curriculum for leadership development?" Our stock answer is "You are the curriculum," to which we generally get a blank stare. But it's true. Effective leaders aren't the product of reading a book, taking a course, or earning a degree. Effective leaders are developed by on-the-job experience and observing the actions of a mentor, who themselves are the primary curriculum. As Jesus demonstrated throughout his ministry, leadership development is mostly hanging out with someone who's worth investing in.

Leadership multiplication is one of the most important ministries church leaders can undertake. It's fundamental both to developing an effective church and building the kingdom. So it's important to take a moment to explain what we mean when we use the word *leadership*.

Definition of Leadership

We define leadership as what a person is able to achieve through other people instead of what they are able to achieve on their own. Leadership is about providing an atmosphere in which people are transformed, equipped, and empowered to be leaders who do God's will. This understanding prompts us to use the metaphor of a spiritual midwife when discussing leadership. Like the midwife who assists parents in the birth of their child, a spiritual midwife assists people in birthing their God-given gifts and in reaching their God-given potential. A spiritual midwife knows that unless a person births their gift they have missed their reason for living.[1]

Leaders are spiritual midwives who help people birth their God-given gifts.

Leadership Assumptions

Our understanding of leadership produces the following assumptions:

- Leadership development must be part of the DNA of all staff and key leaders.
- Every leader must have at least one apprentice.
- A system of discovering and deploying people into a ministry that matches their passion must be in place. It's not enough to just put people into a ministry. They need to be in a ministry for which they have a passion and the gifts to be successful.
- Leadership and discipleship are two sides of the same coin.
- A person's potential is not fixed and can be cultivated. That's why one of the goals of the missional church is for everyone to equip everyone.
- Every person has the potential to be a leader.
- Deploy leaders based on the one person, one passion, one position rule.
- Not all leaders are equal.
- Every organization has multiple levels of leaders.

- Each level of leadership requires a different skill set, value toward work, and application of time. These three aspects of ministry are challenged and changed as a church grows larger. Every time the church grows its leaders have to develop a new skillset, change the way they value getting work done, and adapt the way they spend their time.
- Everyone needs a coach in order to become the kind of leader God designed them to be.
- Process is more important than programs.
- Transforming people into who God intended them to be is more important than simply taking care of people.

Let's take a look at these assumptions to see how they assist in the development of a leadership culture.

Leadership Development Is in the DNA of Every Staff Person and Every Leader

A passion for leadership development must ooze from every pore of the lead pastor as well as from every paid and unpaid leader of the church. Developing leaders isn't just one church program—it's *the* ministry of the church. It's what everyone sheds blood, sweat, and tears over every waking moment, because they know it's the key to building the kingdom rather than merely building a church.

In typical Jerusalem-like churches where the lead pastor is expected to do pastoral ministry, the first step in creating such a leadership culture is to make a pastoral change. This happens in one of two ways. Either the church hires a new pastor who has a passion for leadership development or the current pastor receives an epiphany and begins laying the groundwork for a momentous and significant change. Not only does the lead pastor begin speaking about leadership development at every meeting and quite often in the pulpit, they also begin modeling effective leadership development at every turn.

I (BE) am often asked by churches why they can't develop leaders. To which I always respond, "Tell me what you talk about at your staff meeting." The reason: if you want to develop leaders, you must talk about it. Each staff meeting must have a time when the focus is squarely on leadership development. Our favorite way of explaining this is to suggest that every paid staff person have a "To Be" list that is longer than their "To Do" list. The "To Be" list is comprised of the people each staff person considers to be their apprentices or potential apprentices.

Every Leader Must Have at Least One Apprentice

As a full-blown leadership culture emerges in a church, no one is allowed to lead without having an apprentice. After all, being an apprentice to someone is the very definition of being a disciple. An apprentice is one who is learning a trade. For a disciple, that trade is becoming more like Jesus and living that life among their networks. A leader who doesn't have an apprentice isn't a leader.

Our favorite example of this is New Hope Christian Fellowship in Honolulu, Hawaii. The first time we were there we saw this principle in action. Everywhere we looked, every leader had three or four people they were apprenticing, and in many cases the rank and file were doing the same. For example:

- Many of the people taking up the collection were first-time visitors. They were helping with the offering because they had been brought there by a friend who both embraced and modeled that the church's DNA included "Everyone apprentices someone."
- When we peeked behind the scenes to watch the tech team during the worship service, we saw several people crowded around the person running the slideshow (CGI) learning how to do it for the future.
- Every time we poked our heads into a children's classroom, we saw one or two adults sitting in the corner learning how to teach by watching the teacher.
- Even the snow cone booth had a couple of apprentices learning the trade.

As you can see, leadership multiplication has to become part of the DNA of the church. It must reside in the staff, but it must also reside in every leader and permeate the congregation. As we have said, "You're not a leader unless you are apprenticing someone."

If you can't make it to Hawaii and want to see other examples of a great leadership culture, visit churches like Lake Pointe Church in Rockwall, Texas, or Community Christian Church in Naperville, Illinois. If travel isn't in the cards for you, read *Exponential* by Dave and Jon Ferguson.[2]

A System Must Be in Place for Discovering and Deploying

As a church grows it has to develop a system to discover and deploy new leaders into ministry. No matter where we've consulted, when we find a great leadership culture we discover there is some systematic way of achieving each of the six leadership development processes: (1) identifying, (2) enlisting, (3) equipping, (4) deploying, (5) coaching, and (6) celebrating. In large churches the most difficult processes are identifying, enlisting, and equipping. In small churches the most difficult processes are deploying, coaching, and celebrating. But regardless of your church's size, to be an effective church you must develop a system that encompasses all six processes.

THE CHURCH-LEADERSHIP FARM SYSTEM

What we call the church farm system has proven itself especially effective for discipleship/leadership development. This farm system is loosely based on the one used in professional baseball. Every major league team has a minor league team from which to develop new talent. Each farm system has players, mentors, apprentices, scouts, and coaches. To effectively develop discipled leaders, the church should invest in its own farm system. In a church farm system, the role of the lead pastor is to be the head coach. The lead pastor directly coaches the key leaders and then relies on them to scout and coach the players.

The problem in most churches is that the lead pastor doesn't understand they're a head coach and not a player. A good pastor doesn't play the game (ministry); a good pastor coaches the staff members, who scout and coach others to play the game. The more the lead pastor plays the game, the more dependent the ministry is on the pastor.

But this problem isn't limited to the lead pastor. Most staff make the mistake of playing the game rather than scouting for new players and coaching *them* to play the game. The more the staff insists on playing the game, the fewer number of people are involved in doing actual ministry. Since a staff member can only do so much (for example, a children's pastor can only teach one Sunday school class at a time), the scope of their ministry and their ability to handle additional responsibility is limited. As a church grows, an ineffective staff tries to juggle the increased load, but even the most talented player can only handle so much. Before long something drops, then something else, and soon a chain reaction of failures begins until the ministry unravels completely. This is why so many church plants grow well for a few years but then fall back to a much smaller size. The pastor and/or the staff are stretched beyond their limits for *doing* ministry. Successful church planters learn to hand off ministry from the beginning.

The primary reason most churches never develop a leadership culture is because the lead pastor and/or staff so enjoy playing the game they won't rotate in other players. They rob the congregation of the joy of ministry and reaching their God-given potential.

We're great believers in the axiom that you get what you look for. If someone spends enough time looking for new leaders they will find people willing to be equipped, even in the weakest congregation. God *always* provides what a church needs to be the Church. The problem is our spiritual eyes are too often focused more on accomplishing programs than on discipling people.

A Closer Look at the Leadership Development Team

As we said earlier, every effective leadership culture has a team of players, mentors, apprentices, scouts, and coaches. Let's take a closer look at each.

Players

Players are those who play the game (do hands-on ministry). Everyone plays the game at some level. What is important to note is the *only* time a paid staff person, including the lead pastor, plays the game is when showing an apprentice how the game is played. Beyond that, paid staff should avoid playing the game.

Mentors

Mentors are those players who have shown themselves to be leaders and have an apprentice. Every leader in the church, from committee chairpersons to Sunday school teachers to small group leaders, must be a mentor—and must have an apprentice. There is no leadership without apprenticeship. Therefore, mentors are always keeping their eyes open for promising players and then coming alongside them to raise them up as future leaders.

Mentoring isn't just a matter of teaching or transferring a skill. Effective mentors are active disciplers and they infuse their apprentices with their spiritual values and faith practices.

Apprentices

Apprentices come from all levels of spiritual maturity. The only thing they have in common is a willingness to learn a new skill and be held accountable for using that skill during on-the-job training. This isn't about taking courses or classes, but more like hanging out with their leader (mentor). Most of the time, especially in the beginning, they sit on the bench watching how their leader lives and does ministry. But now and then they get put into the game (leading the ministry). After the game they review the game film with their mentor (talk about how the apprentice did). And then the apprentice returns to the bench to watch until they're called on again.[3]

Scouts

In professional sports, scouts spend much of their time on the road watching high school and college games, looking for raw talent. When they find someone full of promise, they get one of the team's coaches to take a look, after which an offer might be made to procure the new player. In addition, every coach on the team is also looking for prospective players.

It's not much different in the church farm system. Of course a church rarely has a professional scout because in most effective churches it takes more than nine players (and sixteen reserve players) to make a winning team. Therefore, in the church farm system *every* leader and *every* coach plays the role of a scout.

Church scouts are keen observers of their fellow players. They watch for eyes that light up whenever mission is discussed. They look for spiritual hunger and desire for hands-on ministry. And whenever they find someone with promise they let their coaches know. In turn, coaches may take the next step in recruiting by helping connect the player with a mentor (or mentor them themselves).

Coaches

In general, coaches are paid staff. Staff is expected to scout everyone they meet and coach those who are willing to step up to the plate and take a swing at some form of ministry. Then these coaches begin developing them into the best players they can be. In any baseball team there are a variety of coaches: a head coach, pitching coaches, hitting coaches, and base coaches. Similarly, the larger the church the more coaches are necessary because of specialization. A small church might have just a head coach: the lead pastor. A large church will have multiple coaches and perhaps even an assistant coach (a second-in-command, sometimes known as an executive pastor).

Good coaches always have a list of potential replacements in case a starting player gets hurt. In a mature culture of equipping it's not unusual for all key positions to be three or four deep in replacements.

Discipleship Is Leadership Development

Visitors, even first-timers, should be regarded as the potential leaders of the future. In some cases, apprenticeship as a leader will be the journey to becoming a Christian. For instance, the twelve apostles didn't begin their journeys as fully developed believers and disciples; even so, Jesus chose them as his apprentices. As he prepared them for leadership, they came to believe along the way. Therefore, discipleship and leadership development are, in essence, the same ministry. This is especially true in effective church plants where new people come from the ranks of nonbelievers and begin apprenticing as leaders almost immediately. So don't be fooled into thinking leadership development and evangelism aren't twins, because they are.

Leadership Development Is Discipleship

Let's remember that the mission of the church is to make disciples of Jesus Christ. We're not interested in propping up the institutional church for the sake of the institution. The whole point of leadership development is discipleship. The one cannot be separated from the other. Never forget that. As your church invites and retains the unchurched, your leadership culture must also be an environment where new disciples grow in the faith (and long-time disciples become increasingly effective).

When Dave Travis and I (BE) wrote *Beyond the Box* we interviewed Alan Jackson at World Outreach Church in Murfreesboro, Tennessee. When we asked how he measured success, we were blown away by his answer: "By how many ministries we discovered each month for first-time visitors."

What ministries do you have in place for first-time guests and day-old Christians?

A Person's Potential Is Not Fixed and Can Be Cultivated

In a leadership culture every player has the potential of serving as a leader at some level. Therefore a church needs to have different levels of leadership and understand how to move people along the leadership journey. We'll discuss the leadership journey in the next chapter.

Coaches are always asking, "Where is this person today on the leadership journey, and how can we move them further along?" And every time a scout meets a new person, they ponder, "I wonder what gift this person brings that we didn't even know we needed?" That sort of thinking and those kinds of questions change churches.

Every Person Has the Potential to Be a Leader

Believing every person has the potential to be a leader changes everything about the game. It means you see people as God sees them: a special gift to creation just waiting to blossom into all they can be. This understanding of God's gift to humanity underpins any form of effective leadership multiplication. If we truly believe every person is a potential leader, a totally new world of possibilities opens up for a church.

The key is to understand there are various levels of leadership. Not everyone is cut out to be a starting pitcher or a designated hitter— some must manage the equipment, dispense the water, and retrieve the bats. And each position, from superstar pitcher to batboy, needs to be replicated. The effective superstar takes someone under their wing to raise up and encourage, as does the effective batboy. Every position is essential to a winning ball club. In the church, every person is also an essential ingredient to the kingdom. What we are talking about is the metaphor of the human body in 1 Corinthians that describes how *every* Christian plays an indispensable role as part of the body of Christ (see 12:12–17).

The church I (BE) served for twenty-four years had a custodian on staff named Rudy. Rudy had a fifth-grade education. But he had a heart for people and demonstrated that passion on so many occasions that we brought him into the worship center, laid hands on him, and commissioned him, saying, "Take thou the authority to share the gospel." As a result Rudy embraced his calling and led many people to Christ. God uses everyone in his work if we let him.

The One Person, One Passion, One Position Rule

One of the reasons churches can't find the leaders they need is because their leaders "hog the ball." In other words, they don't share well. In many churches, and certainly in most small churches, a single leader may fill several leadership positions. For instance, one person may be a Sunday school teacher, a member of the worship committee, and the treasurer—which means they are probably ex-officio on the finance committee and on the board . . . plus they may sing in the choir. This means three things. First, the leader is overcommitted and unable to give their best to the ministries they're involved in. Second, it means they hold leadership positions that others could, and should, hold. However, it's the third thing that hurts the collective church, the body of Christ, worst of all: the leader's personal passion for their God-called ministry is at best watered down and at worst not nurtured at all.

We are convinced that every person has been given a personal passion—a personal calling—into one ministry or another. When a leader recognizes their passion and is able to pursue it to the exclusion of other tasks, they cannot help but give their best to the effort.

Whenever a leader steps out of their passion, they are robbed of the wonder of ministry and their attention is divided.

The solution is to limit leadership to the passionate . . . and since every person has but one driving passion (they may have multiple interests, but there's only room for one driving passion at any given time), that means they serve in only one leadership role—the one they're passionate about. If each person serves within their passion, and *only* within their passion, that ministry will get their full attention and their best effort. But best of all, it means they'll step aside from other roles so that other leaders can step in.

Sure, we hear the pushback that if someone doesn't do XYZ ministry then it won't get done. We have two responses. First, if there's no one in your church that's called to lead that ministry, then it ought to die anyway; it's not your ministry to do. Second, it begs the question: Do you *really* want someone leading a ministry who isn't passionate about it? God neither calls nor sanctions mediocrity.

Not All Leaders Are Equal

All people are equal in the sight of God, but not all leaders are equal, not even in God's sight. In fact, treating all leaders as if they're equal, even for fairness' sake, is not only unrealistic, it's not biblical. Jesus chose twelve from the crowd to be his apostles. Then he selected Peter, James, and John to be in his inner circle. Ultimately, he charged only Peter to be the keeper of the flock.

Effective coaches invest heavily in those who not only show promise, but who are committed to the leadership journey. That doesn't mean the coach neglects those with less promise or commitment, but with limited time and resources wise leaders invest most heavily where the greatest return can be expected.

Each Leadership Level Is Different

Since we will examine this in detail in the next chapter, all we will say here is that as people move through the leadership journey, what is required of them changes dramatically. Failure to make these necessary adjustments is one of the prime reasons churches plateau.

Everyone Needs a Coach

Since effective leadership development doesn't happen in a classroom but in on-the-job training, a coach is necessary for even the most talented people to reach their maximum leadership potential. Basketball star Michael Jordan was committed to not only having a coach but, as his skills grew, insisted on having the best coach in the business.

Things are changing faster than most pastors have time to assimilate. A coach can help keep them abreast of how the changes are affecting their leadership and help them adapt. In our experience, we've come to the conclusion that the best coaching is more directive than nondirective. In other words, we recommend coaches intervene *before* a leader being coached steps on a land mine that could otherwise be avoided.

Although going too deeply into the coaching process is beyond the scope of this book, the reality is that when it comes to leadership multiplication, the role of the coach cannot be overstated. A coach's role is to help a leader be the best leader they can be. This isn't about helping a leader "think" right, and it's not about teaching good theology. It's about helping a leader achieve their purpose and mission. It's performance-based. Effective leaders are committed to high levels of performance; they want to do better, to do more, to reach their God-given potential. Effective coaches hold leaders accountable to that potential. They "draw out" their best efforts, help them use their strengths while minimizing their weaknesses, and encourage them to stretch further than they've stretched before.

Process Is More Important Than Programs

Most established church people are caught in a program paradigm, so when we talk about scouting for people as part of leadership development, they invariably think we're talking about looking for people to fill program or committee slots for the church. They equate scouting with taking care of the needs of the church's programs, but nothing could be further from what we are saying. We're talking about a lifelong process of developing leaders, not doing programs. When your people grow, the kingdom grows.

At any time, your church may be raising up and mentoring leaders for ministries that don't exist yet. You may be raising up leaders for ministries that are beyond the walls of your church building, or beyond the boundaries of your community, or even beyond your continent. Effective churches raise up leaders for the kingdom, not just leaders for the local church. We must develop for the future, not just for today.

For example, consider churches that start new churches and give people away in the process, churches that develop multiple sites throughout the city, or churches that regularly send out dozens of people to another city to plant a church, like Community Christian Church in Naperville, Illinois. The only way they can achieve such multiplication is because they have a culture of developing leaders. They develop leaders whether or not they need them because they want to see people grow in their faith, not because they want people to run their programs.

Choose Transformation over Caregiving

Every leadership development process we've seen values transforming people over taking care of them. The kicker is you can't transform people if they aren't being cared for to begin with. On the other hand, you *can* take care of people without transforming them. The key is in what you value the most—transformation or caregiving. Merely giving care to healthy people won't result in them becoming all they can become. Leadership development has to go beyond caregiving. Even though it involves taking care of people, the desired end result is always leadership and discipleship.

Elevate Others Even If It Means They Outgrow You

One of the greatest joys I (BE) have had in ministry is watching people I've mentored go on to achieve greater success in their ministry than I did. Two of the associate pastors I was fortunate enough to scout out and mentor over a period of years have gone on to great success.

If you've been following my consulting ministry you know I took Tom Bandy on as a partner more than ten years ago. I was doing a speaking tour in Canada for a denomination and they were afraid I couldn't speak Canadianese, so they sent Tom along with me to interpret. As we did the tour, Tom would show me diagrams he was making as a result of what I was saying. After a couple of weeks, I said to him, "Why don't you do some of the speaking at the next stop? Your diagrams are great." By the time the tour was over Tom was doing quite a bit of the speaking. A couple of years went by, during which time I kept getting letters from Tom that were so elegant you could publish them. So I began to bug him to write a book. It took more than two years, but in time he published his bestseller *Kicking Habits* and used the diagrams he drew on the tour as the basis for much of the book. Later we did two tours in the United States and Tom was on his way. Remember the "You do; I watch; we talk" we spoke of earlier? Well, this is how it works in real life.

Fractals and Leadership Multiplication

Throughout this book we decry the reality that most staff, and in truth many pastors, are more doers (players) than leaders (coaches). In chapter 3 we introduced you to the four core processes and how to staff them. This illustrated how the lead pastor must ultimately move from doing ministry to doing ministry *through* the eyes, hands, and feet of the four key leaders. By delegating these four processes, the lead pastor has effectively been multiplied (four key leaders are now responsible for virtually everything the lead pastor is ultimately responsible for). In this section we're going to expand upon how the fractal model should work in the church to effectively multiply leaders. Again, remember that this model is scalable; a church with less than one hundred in worship can use the fractal paradigm as effectively as a church of fifteen thousand or even larger. The differences will primarily be who is paid staff and who is not. However, leaders of churches with less than three hundred on average in worship should pay careful attention to chapters 9–11 before jumping into the arduous task of reorganizing and reconfiguring their current leadership structure.

There is nothing magical about the number four, yet we've found in most cases any one core process can be broken naturally into four subprocesses. Let's expand the Retain Them process as we would expect to see it built in a growing church. As we mentioned earlier, the four subprocesses (or responsibilities) of the Retain Them core process are: welcoming hospitality, worship that connects, follow-up, and friend-making. This is graphically represented in the following diagram.

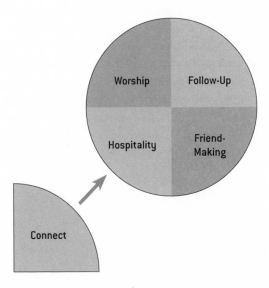

When the Connect key leader is hired, their first order of business is to evaluate the Retain Them core process to ascertain whether the subprocesses recommended are indeed the ones that would best serve the local congregation. Once that's been settled, the next step is to begin looking for four leaders whose passions closely match the processes. For instance, we expect that the worship leader would step into the Worship subprocess. A leader passionate about hospitality would step into the Hospitality subprocess. And so on.

In a smaller church, the four Retain Them subprocess leaders might be people who are primarily players; that is, they are the ones responsible for "doing" that ministry. However, as the church grows it will be critical that these players either grow to become coaches or their position is replaced (e.g., though the player might keep right on doing ministry, a coach would step into their former position). In any event, once the Connect key leader has scouted and recruited leaders for all four Retain Them subprocesses, they should no longer be "doing" ministry but spending most of their time coaching their fractal leaders and scouting for future leaders. This transition is every bit as difficult as it is for the lead pastor to make—so pastor, plan on spending significant time coaching your key leaders in hands-off ministry leading.

But we're not done. Multiplying leaders won't necessarily end at this level. The larger the church, the deeper the fractals go. So let's continue our example with one more level—the Friend-Making subprocess (see the diagram below). You'll notice that the Friend-Making leader designed their fractal structure around key opportunities for connecting people with one another: Small Groups, Fellowship Opportunities, Short-Term Classes, and Events. The Friend-Making leader will eventually need to find committed and passionate players or coaches who will take the responsibility for doing these ministries.

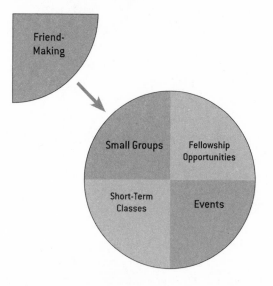

Just like the Connect key leader, who may begin their position "doing" some hands-on ministry, ultimately each fractal leader will fill each process and will have to step into a more active coaching role or else be replaced. This same process is repeated as the church grows. For instance, the Events leader may develop their fractal with (1) Community Events, (2) Mission Events, (3) Mixers, and (4) Sports/Recreation. And so it goes.

The key to effective fractaling is the one person, one passion, one position rule we mentioned earlier. If each process is led by someone whose primary passion is in play, you can rest assured the ministry will flourish. But here's the real payoff. Notice the multiplication of leaders via the Connect key leader (see the diagram below). As the church grows the number of leaders increases exponentially; in this case the coaching and scouting work of the Connect key leader has expanded to include twenty-eight additional leaders. And if each of the key leaders are effective coaches and scouts, that means there would be 112 committed and passionate coaches and players each doing their part for the kingdom.

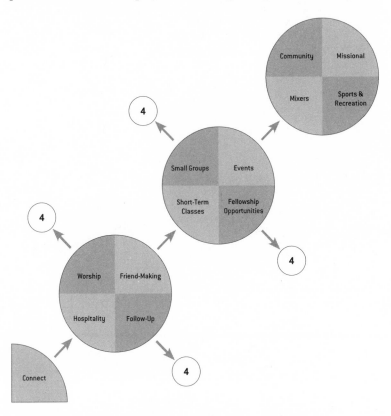

When it comes to leadership development, we've found it helpful to establish a leadership process that all the staff knows how to use. That's the subject of the next two chapters.

9

The Leadership Journey

No one told me (BE) I had to grow along with the growth of my church. No one told me there would be times when I would have to undergo huge and often traumatic changes in the way I functioned if I wanted to keep up with the growth of the church. I didn't have any training in how to pastor. Seminary didn't teach me how to lead. No one was around to mentor me. There weren't any churches in my area to show me the way into the emerging new world. I'd never heard of people like Lyle Schaller. I was on my own.

Ever feel this way?

In 1969, I (BE) was appointed to a restart situation and I had to learn to swim with the sharks or be eaten alive. Over the next twenty-four years I went through four gut-wrenching changes in my journey to be the leader God needed for that size church. And over the past twenty years of consulting, working with many world-class leaders, I've honed what I call "the leadership journey." I refer to leadership growth as a journey because leadership development is most often a messy process of two steps forward and one step back. In this chapter we will examine three different versions of the leadership journey.

The Traditional Leadership Journey

The further into the leadership journey a person goes, the more skills that are required. As you can see in the diagram below, when people

Traditional Leadership Journey

demonstrate dependability and effectiveness they are offered more responsibility based on their gifts and level of commitment.

Four types of leaders make up the traditional leadership journey:

1. Those who are the leader of leaders. In most churches this is a short list that includes a lead pastor or an executive pastor who oversees staff. However, in those churches that have a robust leadership culture, every staff member is a leader of leaders, as are many key unpaid leaders.

2. Those who oversee long-term ministries such as Sunday school or a small group system. These people are usually full-time paid staff. They are required to oversee and develop the leaders for ministries that cover more than one season in the life of a church, so these people must have staying power.

3. Those who oversee short-term ministries such as Vacation Bible School or Alpha. These people are usually unpaid staff or part-time paid staff. They are required to oversee and develop the leaders of ministries that have a short duration but are still considered essential to the life of the congregation.

4. Those who chair committees. In a *thriving* church, chairing a committee normally means leading some sort of ministry planning and implementation team. However, in most churches leading a committee means holding too many meetings, discussing agenda items for too long, and at best making a recommendation so

someone else who has authority can make a decision or at worst prolonging a decision until it's too late to make a significant difference. Therefore this position is the least important position in a thriving church and is usually led by an unpaid person.

Each destination along the journey requires a different skillset, work value, and application of time. Each destination plays a part in the journey, but some destinations require more from the leader than others. We will discuss these differences in the next chapter.

The Indigenous Leadership Journey

The indigenous leadership journey usually focuses its key leaders primarily on worship and small groups rather than on a variety of long- and short-term ministries. It is also not uncommon for this journey to be without most, if not all, committees found in the traditional model. Many churches on this journey believe "less is best," so they have streamlined what they do and how they govern.

Indigenous Leadership Journey

The Multi-Site Leadership Journey

Two additional leadership positions are added in this version of the leadership journey: campus pastor and church planter. Adding these two positions exponentially escalates the need to multiply the number of mature people in ministry. In many cases, the ultimate goal of these churches is to spawn a movement of multi-sites and/or churches that plant churches.

Multi-Site Leadership Journey

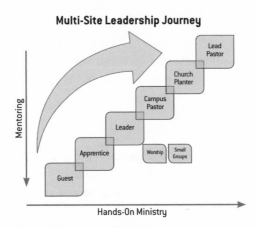

This version of the leadership journey also focuses more on worship and small groups than long- and short-term ministries and committees. Whereas they may have a few long- and short-term ministries, churches that use the leadership journey to spawn multiple campuses focus so much of their attention on multiplication of locations that they learn less is best and tend to do more ministries in the community and fewer ministries within the church building.

If you're the pastor of a church with less than five hundred in worship, the next chapter will be critical for your personal leadership journey. On the other hand, if you lead a church with over five hundred in worship you can probably skip the next chapter . . . unless you find yourself working over fifty hours a week trying to juggle ministries, ministry leaders, and life.

10

The Leadership Journey for the Solo Pastor and the Smaller Church

If you're a solo pastor who's picked up this book in order to prepare yourself for what's ahead in your career, you might be a bit overwhelmed with things like core processes, key leaders, and the like. Indeed, if you read carefully between the lines you might even conclude that we've minimized the leap in average worship from one hundred to five hundred plus. And we'll be brutally honest: in some ways you'd be correct.

Don't get us wrong; we know that the single most difficult ceiling to break in the church is the two hundred barrier. Even conservative statistics show that over 80 percent of all churches that try to break through two hundred end up failing—and the failure rate is even higher for mainline churches. But here's the reality: *staffing alone won't grow your church through this barrier, and neither will great pastoral leadership.* The reason it's so difficult for a small church to make it to three hundred or more is because it requires both a mind shift and a major behavioral change not only for the pastor, but for both the formal and informal congregational leaders as well.

Acknowledging the Brick Ceiling

In the next chapter we'll begin discussing the leadership journey for the pastor. We want to make it clear that we believe everything depends on leadership, and specifically on the leadership of the lead pastor. However, in churches that haven't broken the two hundred barrier we've found that in many, if not most, of these churches the issue isn't necessarily the pastor. We don't know how many under-two-hundred churches we've consulted with who've had a steady stream of "bad" pastors unable to "grow" the church. In desperation the church calls on us and asks if we can help them find that rare leader who can help them break two hundred. It's difficult to be politically correct in these cases. For the *vast* majority of these churches, the problem has not been their pastoral leadership—the congregation itself has been the immovable brick ceiling that has stymied sustainable growth.[1]

It Takes a Congregation to Grow a Church

Breaking the almighty two hundred barrier demands a cooperative effort between lead pastor and the congregation. Although we're sure some will criticize the following task list as simplistic and unrealistic, we've yet to find a church able to break the brick ceiling without taking the following journey.

> To illustrate our point about the brick ceiling, let us tell you about a small church we helped take a step forward. I (BE) was asked by a church running seventy-five in worship to help them reach more young adults. So I helped them start a second worship service geared toward adults under age forty. Eighteen months later the church was running 140 in worship. You would think they would be happy with the results, but they weren't. They cancelled the new service, fired the pastor, and returned to one service thinking all would be well. But it wasn't. In two years the church closed because it had made everyone mad.
>
> The reason they cancelled the new service? The new service had 120 people in it, and the longstanding traditional service was down to twenty people all over the age of sixty—and they controlled the purse strings.

1. *Pastoral Leadership Point.* The pastor hands off virtually all ministry in order to invest 70 to 80 percent of their time networking, inviting, and connecting with the unchurched.

   Congregational Response. The congregational leaders not only allow and encourage the pastor's inviting efforts, but they run interference from those who would shackle the pastor to the office or to other membership ministries.

2. *Pastoral Leadership Point.* The pastor spends their remaining time training, not just teaching, the congregation to invite and integrate new people into the church.

   Congregational Response. The congregational leaders not only allow and encourage the pastor's relentless efforts to launch invitation initiatives within the congregation, they model inviting and integrating new people into their lives and into the life of the church. When the average worship attendance doubles, the congregational leaders refuse to be threatened by the possibility that they may be outvoted and/ or may lose "control" of their church. In fact, not only do they model confidence in their pastor and in the direction of the church, they become a calming influence to those in the congregation who become uncomfortable with "not knowing everybody" and/or any other possible concern that would otherwise stymie continued growth.

Reality Check

Fact: most churches fail to break the two hundred barrier because they cannot embrace the reality that the church doesn't exist for *their* sake, but for the sake of those who are not there yet. Until the pastor, the church leaders, and the congregation as a whole refocus their attention from themselves to those beyond their walls, they will not be able to see significant and sustainable growth. Instead they will grow until they reach approximately double their current size and then one of two things will happen. In the majority of churches conflict will break out and the average worship attendance will fall back to its original size. In a smaller number of churches the church will grow through the barrier because the pastor and/or possibly the staff not

*Fact: most churches
fail to break the
two hundred barrier
because they cannot
embrace the reality
that the church doesn't
exist for their sake, but
for the sake of those
who are not there yet.*

only grow the church but also provide strong pastoral care; in other words, they grow the church by inviting, but they also continue to do hands-on ministry. In these cases, it isn't long before the pastor or staff member responsible for the growth burns out, contracts a protracted illness or disease, or has a moral failure that either forces their removal or at least renders them ineffective. When this happens the church returns to its previous size.

Becoming Part of the 20 Percent

The 20 percent of churches that beat the odds and break the two hundred brick ceiling do so because they are more committed to the kingdom than anything else. Collectively they're willing to sacrifice personal comfort, status quo "We've always done it this way," and even the loss of some long-term members who won't make the sacrifice to be effective followers of Christ. They're not willing to sacrifice their mission, compromise their values, or adulterate their vision.

It's a lot easier to say these words than it is to bid a charter member Godspeed when they quit the church because they're hurt and angry that the pastor chose to spend time with somebody no one in the congregation knew rather than visiting the charter member when they had knee-replacement surgery. But those are exactly the kind of choices that grow the kingdom of God—and grow churches through the two hundred brick ceiling. With that in mind, you may understand why 80 percent of churches trying to break two hundred fail.

Staffing the Four Processes in Any Size Church

For the would-be 20 percent, the leadership journey begins with the commitment to break the brick ceiling, but it also takes seriously the four core processes and staffing for growth. We realize that the average church in North America has fewer than sixty people in worship each week, so after reading the previous chapters you may be feeling a bit overwhelmed. After all, we've told you that the four processes are at the core of an effective church and we've made it abundantly clear that asking a volunteer to be the primary person responsible for *any* of them is foolish . . . and then we turned around and told you that the pastor's primary responsibility is inviting new folks and letting go of almost everything else. So that begs the question: How do you get everything covered?

The following section illustrates how a small church of under two hundred in worship can staff for growth and navigate the transitions. Keep in mind that growing a church from less than fifty in attendance to over five hundred is not as easy as we're going to make it sound—there's that brick ceiling between here and there. But let us assure you that it is a very *simple* process . . . and it's a process that has been tested and proven again and again and again.

Staffing under One Hundred

In churches with fewer than a hundred in average worship, the solo pastor is responsible for the four core processes, but not in equal proportions. We realize that's a lot of responsibility and we don't want to minimize the load this puts on the pastor. Indeed, this is the precise reason most churches never get beyond one hundred in worship. It's not because the responsibility of the core processes is too much . . . that particular load, though heavy, is quite bearable. It's all the other expectations and responsibilities that church members pile onto their pastor that make the core processes unbearable.

If your church is serious about reaching the community for Jesus Christ then it will have to release the pastor to devote his or her attention to the core processes, with the majority of their energy and time devoted to Invite and Connect, and to stop doing almost everything else. This means someone else will have to create the bulletin, write the newsletter, and make most of the hospital and membership visits. It means that the pastor's "office" hours are replaced with "out in the community connecting with the unchurched" hours. Monthly committee meetings may need to become quarterly, semiannual, annual . . . or cancelled altogether.[2] As we've already said, the most important

91

thing a pastor does at this size church is bring people through the front door and then follow up with every guest. The most important thing a church does at this size is support its pastor's efforts. The second most important thing it does is follow the pastor's lead to create an inviting culture. But all of that will be wasted unless the church is committed to welcoming and adopting all those new people into the congregation.

Staffing for Growth: The First Hire

One of the axioms to growing a church is that creating space for growth always *precedes* significant growth. In other words, you have to be ready for growth before it will happen. For instance, if you want to attract young families you'll need to get your nursery up to snuff *before* they visit—it's too late if they show up and your nursery is filled with leftover toys and recalled cribs.

The same is true for staffing your church. You'll need to invest in your first hire *before* you can comfortably afford it. If you're a leader in a small church, you might as well start preparing your congregation to get used to that kind of stretch . . . it's going to be this way for the rest of time. Effective staffing is an investment that's paid off in the future, not in the present. With that said, when your congregation passes about one hundred in average worship it's time to become a multi-staff church.

The first hire is where the vast majority of small churches shoot themselves in the foot. At the one hundred level you're bound to hear, "We need a youth leader because the youth are the future of our church." There's nothing further from the truth. Consider:

- No self-respecting unchurched fourteen-year-old wants their parents to attend *anything* they're involved in, let alone their church.
- Youth grow up—and the vast majority not only move away from the community, they leave the church. Sadly, it's not only your church they leave. Recent studies have shown that even youth raised in the church leave when they become young adults and don't return to church even after they're married and have children.[3]

- Even with a full-time youth pastor, a small church cannot effectively "compete" with the youth programming of the "big church" up the street, whether that's a church of three hundred or three thousand. If a family is church shopping for a church based on youth programming, a small church doesn't stand a chance.

The fact is, parents bring youth to church, not the other way around. So if you want to grow your church, the first hire you must make is one that will both attract and retain your mission target (your "audience"). We *always* recommend that a church's first hire be a worship pastor/leader.

Hiring a good worship pastor/leader does four things for the church. First, it expands the possibility of indigenous services for multiple target audiences (a must for most small churches that are committed to sustainable church growth). Second, it increases the level of excellence of all the services, which pays off in more excitement in the congregation. More excitement means more invitations to friends, relatives, acquaintances, neighbors, co-workers, and everyone else. And of course, more invitations boosts the number of first-time guests. Third, as new indigenous services increase, so does the retention rate of first-time guests who hang around long enough to become effective disciples of Jesus Christ. And finally, it frees up the lead pastor to spend less time in worship development and more time in networking with the unchurched and helping them find connections within the congregation.

Staffing for the Next Level

There are only two ministries that virtually guarantee church growth for the smaller church: indigenously targeted, quality worship that reaches younger adults and excellent children's ministry. The axiom "Momma decides where the family will go to church and the kids decide if they go back" is as true today as it was in the '50s when the phrase was coined. Get the family in with great worship. Keep them coming back with great children's programming.

As a church grows toward two hundred in average worship, it's time to staff for the next level, which means hiring a children's pastor/

leader. The key to this hire is to make sure you're hiring a leader, not a doer. The children's pastor's job is to create high-quality, fun, disciple-making ministries that children can't wait to return to. Their job isn't to lead a Sunday school class, do a children's sermon during worship, or chaperone the kids at an all-church picnic. In fact, if either of us came across our children's pastor leading a Sunday school class, they'd better have a really good reason why there wasn't an adult volunteer leading the class, or else they'd be looking for another job. The children's pastor must be a leader of leaders who accomplishes ministry through the hands and feet of committed servants and volunteers. By so doing, the children's pastor will have the ability to remain effective regardless of the church's size.

With just three ministry staff members (lead pastor, worship pastor, and children's pastor) the church should expect to see sustainable growth through three hundred. Of course there are many factors that can stymie a church's sustained growth, but almost all of them are internal issues. Very rarely do external issues such as a declining community, eroding economics, persecution, or cultural apathy keep churches from growing. In fact, we know of churches located where towns "used to be" that are not only sustainable, but experiencing significant growth. There are churches in city centers standing toe-to-toe with urban blight that continue to break attendance barriers. And there are churches in every other nook and cranny of North America that are experiencing growth. Almost every church that complains there are outside reasons why they aren't growing is making excuses for their less than effective behaviors. When a mission-focused congregation follows committed, well-trained, mentored, and coached staff, there's no reason a church can't move through the "next level" and into sustainable effectiveness.

Staffing for Sustainable Effectiveness

You may notice that up until this point we've primarily tasked the lead pastor with gathering new folks. Indeed, we maintain that until a church breaks five hundred in average worship the lead pastor's first priorities are to (1) meet new people, (2) build initial relationships with them, (3) get them into the church for worship or an event, (4) follow up with them, (5) help them connect with a small group, (6) hand off their care to the small group leader, and (7) repeat.

However, at the 350–500 level it's time for the lead pastor to let go of one of the four core processes by hiring the first key leader. Although each of the core processes is important, the Connect key leader is generally the most effective first key leader hire. The reason for this is simple: since both worship and small groups (including children's ministry) fall within the Retain Them process, the Connect key leader will bring some immediate relief to an overworked lead pastor. Not that the lead pastor suddenly gets a break. From here on out the lead pastor must radically begin shifting practices and priorities from *doing* to *leading*, which is the focus of the rest of this book.

After the Connect key leader, the next three hires are based on need. It's important that the lead pastor hires around their weakness. If the lead pastor has been exceptional at apprenticing new leaders, but not too good in marketing, then the next key leader could be the Invite key leader. On the other hand, if the church has a budding signature outreach ministry, then it might be wise to hire the Send key leader. During this season it is often particularly helpful to seek wise counsel, and many churches that successfully navigate this important transition do so with the guidance of a seasoned consultant and coach.

Through the next chapters we'll examine how the leadership journey works out in the lives of a pastor and staff.

11

The Leadership Journey
for the Lead Pastor

It's next to impossible to find a thriving church today without a strong pastor at the helm, much less find a movement of leadership development and multiplication without strong leaders. So we need to examine how the leadership journey plays out in the life of a pastor and staff as they move along the journey from a small to large church context.

Leadership Journey for Pastors

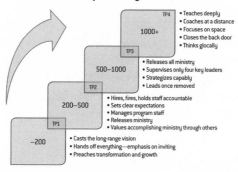

As you can see in the above diagram, every effective pastor goes through a series of four transition points (TPs) as the church grows in size. Some pastors traverse these transition points intuitively, but most pastors have to learn the hard way. This is where a coach enters the picture. The right coach can make the transitions smoother and more effective.

Three Fundamental Shifts

Moving through each transition point requires three fundamental shifts in the life of the lead pastor.[1] Each of these transitions is absolutely necessary for the lead pastor to make if they are going to grow a church significantly—and each of these transitions is exceptionally difficult for most traditionally trained pastors. Please pay careful attention to each. Let's take a quick look at all three, and then come back to them later. Every transition point requires a change in:

The Pastor's Skillset. The skillset changes from jack-of-all-trades to managing staff, thinking strategically, being visionary, and thinking glocally. At this stage in the development of the congregation's size it becomes important that the church thinks and acts both locally and globally, thus the term *glocal.*[2]

The Pastor's Values. The basic value shift is centered on the belief that it is better to coach others to do ministry than do it yourself. What a pastor believes about the *role* of the pastor is paramount to growing an effective church. If they only value the ministry they can achieve, the mission is stifled. If they value getting ministry done through other people, the church thrives.

The Pastor's Time Management. The larger the church becomes, the less time the pastor spends on the church and the more time is spent on self-improvement, staff, leadership development, and networking. As the church grows, the staff has to become much more specialized in what they do.

Introducing the Four Transition Points

As you will see in these next four chapters, there are several transition points a church, staff, and pastor go through as the church grows. Each transition point (TP) is based on the size of the church, and requires a new skillset, a change in how work is valued, and how time is applied. We have chosen to walk the reader through the first four transition points, since few churches grow beyond two thousand in worship.

In order to get a better grip on this leadership journey, the next four chapters will explore the concepts through the life and times of a pastor named Jim as he travels through these four transition points.

12

The Journey through Transition Point One

Jim's first church right out of seminary was in a rural area of the Midwest. He was the staff. If something was going to get done, Jim had to do it—or at least that's what the church members expected, and it was what he'd been taught. It wasn't long, however, before Jim found himself becoming frustrated with the whole situation. He was working seventy to eighty hours a week, but most of those hours were spent either in the office, attending one committee meeting after another, or driving to one of the regional hospitals to visit church members or their extended family. First-time guests in worship were almost nonexistent, and those who came rarely returned. Even worse, in Jim's mind, according to the church records there hadn't been an adult baptism for years, even though less than 40 percent of the county attended any church.

Up until this point, Jim had relied on seminary training and his experiences growing up in the church to be his "How to Lead a Church" guide. He turned to a colleague who was in a growing church for advice. "You can't do this on your own," his friend said. "Get yourself a good coach." Jim was pretty sure he'd already learned everything he needed to know about growing a church, but after a couple of months of seventy-five-hour weeks and no new members, he became desperate and hired a coach.

From that moment on his life and ministry were never the same. It literally changed his life. Jim had taken the first step on the leadership journey and TP1 (see the diagram below).

Leadership Journey for Pastors

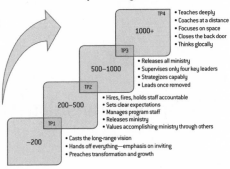

The first thing the coach helped Jim see was that he was working too many hours and was robbing the congregation of the joy of serving and growing in their own discipleship. Next the coach opened his eyes to the two essential ingredients for personally growing along with the church. One, Jim discovered his legacy would not be measured by *what* he left behind but by *whom* he left behind. Two, his coach also helped him realize that the more ministry he handed off to others, the more potential for growth there was for the individual, the church, and the kingdom. Over time Jim learned to apply these two ingredients to his ministry and both the church and its people began to grow.

The Difficulty in Making the TP1 Transition

The transition from being a solo pastor who believes that if something is going to get done the pastor has to do it to getting ministry done through other people is the single most difficult transition in the life of a leader. It's one thing to be a competent jack-of-all-trades; it's another to know how to get ministry done through other people. You know what you can count on from yourself; you don't know what you can count on from others until they prove themselves. But if a pastor doesn't learn to hand off ministry, one of the following happens: the pastor burns out; the pastor gets a divorce; the pastor quits ministry; or the pastor settles for what they can accomplish alone, the church remains small, the people never mature, and late in life the pastor, who wanted to be effective, is filled with regret. If the pastor gets this first transition down, the rest comes much easier.

Jim's problem was he hadn't understood that *everything* about him as a leader had to change as the church grew. He'd gone to seminary to learn how to *do* ministry, not how to be a "CEO" kind of leader who accomplished ministry through the hands and feet of others. He had valued being hands-on and intricately involved with everything going on. He found it hard to hand off ministry to others for two reasons. First, because the church leaders assured him that they'd hired *him* to do the ministry. Second, he also enjoyed *doing* ministry (which of course kept the church leaders happy). He so enjoyed playing the game he found it hard to become a scout and a coach—besides, he worried about making waves. He'd never entertained the notion that everyone in his church had the potential to be an accountable leader, much less that someone might be capable of doing ministry as well or better than he could. Jim discovered he would have to change his core values and help the congregation change theirs if he was to achieve his God-given dream.

The Change in Skillset

Moving through TP1 requires, at minimum, that the pastor have the ability to:

- Cast the church's long-range vision
- Focus preaching on transformation and growth
- Be responsible for all four core processes, but focus on Invite
- Hand off ministry to unpaid leaders
- Hold unpaid leaders accountable
- Learn to hire and fire people—both paid and unpaid

Let's take a look at these.

Casts the Church's Long-Range Vision

There is no skill more important than having the ability to perceive and effectively communicate a church's vision. If a pastor cannot move, touch, and inspire their congregation to move toward a preferred future, then nothing else we write is going to make any difference. This is as true in a twelve-member church as it is in a thirty-thousand-member church. If you're just a *good* communicator, take a couple of public speaking courses and join Toastmasters to move from good to great. If people's eyes don't light up when you share the church's vision in conversation, get some training, such as the Dale Carnegie Course. Do *whatever* you have to do to become a great proponent and communicator of the church's vision. Otherwise it's all over before you even start.

Focuses on Invite

Although at this point the pastor is responsible for all four core processes, the number one all-consuming process must be Invite. As we've said, this means the pastor must spend 70 to 80 percent of their time beyond the walls of the church networking, meeting, and connecting with the unchurched and with church guests.

But it's not enough for the pastor to be an inviter; the pastor must train the rest of the congregation to invite as well. The creation of an inviting culture cannot be overstated. Virtually every sermon, every Bible study, and every meeting must somehow be focused and framed as an Invite training session. But remember, the most effective "sermon" is for the pastor to not only model inviting, but to show results from their invitations.

Hands Off Ministry

If the pastor is faithful in inviting and in taking seriously excellence in communicating the vision, that means there isn't a whole lot of time left to lead other ministries. Therefore it's critical for the pastor to take their cue from Paul's words to the Ephesians:

> So Christ himself gave the apostles, the prophets, the evangelists, the pastors and teachers, to equip his people for works of service, so that the body of Christ may be built up. (4:11–12)

The key phrase is "to equip his people for works of service." This isn't a license for the pastor to get lazy and not get their hands dirty in mission and ministry, but it does mean that their core job is getting the church to take responsibility for doing ministry. We know this isn't easy, but in our experience if a pastor doesn't learn how to recruit, resource, empower, and coach unpaid leaders to do hands-on ministry, they won't be any better at managing paid staff.

Warning: if you decide what's really important is to recruit, mentor, train, empower, deploy, and coach leaders to do ministry, you'll never break two hundred, let alone move through TP1. Instead, you'll spend all your hours with church members, discipling them. Your first priority must be to invite, invite, train to invite, and invite some more. When someone in the congregation steps up and is willing to do an existing ministry, and if they're willing to be held accountable for the results of that ministry, then by all means help them into that ministry. You should be able to hand off things like hospital visitation within a couple of visits—take someone with you and have them watch, have them do it while you watch the next time, then ask them to take someone else with them the next time. Voila! You've handed it off. When worship size approaches 150–175, you'll need to become more diligent at scouting and recruiting leaders so you can let go of more and more ministry. And by the time you get to 200–225, you should be pretty good at it. But no matter what, your number one priority, even at 250, is inviting. If anything gets in the way of that, the game's all over.

Embraces Accountability

Getting unpaid leaders to do hands-on ministry is only the start. It's much easier to get someone to agree to take on a ministry than it is to hold them accountable for leading with excellence. The key to success here is being absolutely clear about expectations *before* putting a new ministry leader into a position and then holding them accountable for meeting those expectations. Learning how to be both an effective mentor and a coach will be the difference between success and abject failure.

Holding someone accountable doesn't mean holding a club over their head. But it *does* mean keeping them focused on what they

Delegation and empowerment are not the same.

were asked to do and getting them the resources to accomplish it. Accountability means evaluating how the ministry leader is fitting in with the team, whether or not they're reaching their goals, and whether they're growing in their position.

How a pastor holds someone accountable is based on how they go about handing off ministry. There are two ways to hand off ministry: delegation and empowerment. If the pastor uses delegation, accountability is more direct and frequent. Delegation sounds something like this, depending on the acquired trust level between the ministry leader and pastor:

- "Here is something I want you do to; keep me informed every step of the way."
- "Here is something I want you to do; keep me in the loop."
- "Here is something I want you to do; come see me if you have problems."

Note that in each case the leader spells out what needs to be done. Although this is a tried-and-proven way to get a job done, it rarely multiplies ministry and it never sees a ministry reach its full potential, because it is tied to the supervisor's apron strings. This isn't quite micromanaging, but it's only a hairsbreadth away. However, this is where the pastor generally starts because they may not be "sure" about the ministry leader's abilities.

Empowerment has far less direct accountability and requires that the ministry leader has proven to be trustworthy and to have integrity—they do what they say they're going to do by when they say they're going to do it. Empowerment provides an exponential environment, but it still requires feedback and oversight. Empowerment sounds something like this:

- "I trust you to reach our agreed-upon goals. Just let me know how it goes and holler if you need something. Let's get together next month to see how it's going."

The key to both delegation and empowerment is not to abdicate accountability and feedback after handing off the ministry. Availability is one of the most important resources a pastor can offer. If after six months a ministry leader isn't performing at the level expected, they will need to be removed from the position, which brings us to the next skill.

Learns to Hire and Fire

As we pointed out earlier, when the church reaches about one hundred in worship it's about time to make the first staff hire. This is when the pastor gets their first real shot at hiring and firing staff. However, it's at this level that the pastor will have to learn the difficult task of removing ministry leaders from their positions. We're not talking about removing board members from their positions (good luck with that), but "inviting" the newsletter editor to step down because they have consistently missed deadlines, or helping "relocate" the Vacation Bible School chair when they refuse or are unable to play as a team member.

Whether you're using delegation or empowerment, you can't abdicate supervision.

We realize that this is a difficult skill to learn. It seems that most pastors have a high spiritual gift of mercy, and it can seem almost cutthroat to relieve a ministry leader of their responsibilities. However in many, if not most, cases the reason the ministry leader has been unsuccessful is because they're in a position for which they have little passion (see chapter 8 for more on the one passion, one position practice). Helping someone out of a position for which they are poorly suited may be the kindest thing you can do for them.

The Change in Values

In the early stages of his ministry Jim valued doing ministry himself. However, to successfully move through TP1, Jim had to see helping other people succeed in ministry as the prize to be valued. Jim had to learn that the role of the pastor is not doing ministry, but equipping others to do ministry. Remember, leadership is not about how much a person accomplishes in their lifetime; leadership is about multiplying the number of people in ministry. Effective leaders change lives. They ask: "Are people transformed? Are they finding their place in God's world? Are they passing that on to others?" The multiplication of one's self is the key to fulfilling the kingdom and the key to moving through TP1.

One of the most important lessons we've learned is that as the lead pastor your primary vocational responsibility is to the kingdom first, the church second, and individuals last. This means that if *any* individual is hindering the church from reaching its potential, that individual either has to change or they have to be removed. Sometimes this means you'll have the unsavory task of firing someone. It also means there will be times you'll have the heartbreaking task of inviting a layperson to find another church. No one person, not even a small group of persons, can be allowed to derail the work, mission, and ministry of the church.

The Change in Time Management

As a solo pastor, Jim spent most of his time taking care of the church members. Much of his time was spent going to hospitals, visiting shut-ins, and attending meetings. When Jim learned the value of equipping the congregation for ministry, much of his time shifted from taking care of people to transforming and equipping them. Jim found himself taking people with him to the hospital and mentoring them in how to do hospital visitation. In time he turned that ministry over to those he'd trained. The same thing happened in the ministry to shut-ins. And instead of going to an endless round of meetings, Jim shifted to spending several evenings a week visiting first-time visitors. In addition, he discovered that he really didn't need to be at every meeting every time. Instead, he learned to trust the church leaders to remain true to the mission of the church, and when they didn't he found a way to remove them.

By handing off ministry one piece at a time, Jim was able to spend more time inviting new people. The more new people who came, the more new leaders stepped up. And the more leaders he had, the more time he could invest in them to ensure ministry was done well . . . which gave him even more time to invite and to train others to invite. And so the circle went.

Living the Priorities

You may be wondering how the lead pastor is going to spend all those hours they've gained now that staff (and laity) are doing the lion's share of the church's hands-on ministry. The answer is simple. If the church has less than three hundred in average worship attendance, then the lead pastor should be spending 70 to 80 percent of their time doing the following:

- Helping integrate first-time guests and returning guests into the congregation
- Spending time in the community networking and relationship-building with the unchurched, and in particular the unchurched who match the congregation's target member/audience
- Attending parties, functions, meals, and so forth with members and their unchurched friends in order to network and build relationships with the unchurched

If it sounds like the lead pastor spends most of their time with people who aren't church members, that's correct. Moving successfully through TP1 necessitates a hearty helping of church growth.

Early Signs of Failure to Move through TP1

- Inability to rally congregational leaders behind the church's vision
- Being distracted from continually gathering new people
- Inability to increasingly hand off ministries
- Inability to articulate clear expectations to ministry leaders

- Inability to hold ministry leaders accountable to clear expectations
- Inability to remove ministry leaders who cannot perform

At this point Jim has successfully navigated the first leadership transition point. As we've mentioned earlier this is by far the most difficult transition for most lead pastors to make. But his journey has just begun.

13

The Journey through Transition Point Two

Having successfully navigated the first transition point, Jim saw his congregation experience significant growth and he was called to a church that averaged almost 350 in weekend services. Again he felt like a fish out of water. He had just learned how to work with a small staff; now he was asked to work with a staff that included a full-time worship leader, children's leader, and youth leader, not to mention several other part-time staff members. Clearly, Jim was in unfamiliar territory. Once again he turned to his coach.

The first thing Jim's coach told him was that just because a church was averaging over three hundred didn't mean it had broken the brick ceiling. Many churches this size remain organized and operate as if they were pastor-centered. It would be necessary for Jim to renew his commitment to the skills, values, and time management he'd learned navigating TP1. In addition, Jim's coach shared that his future success would depend more on how he managed staff than on anything else. If Jim was going to reach his goals he would have to gather a group of passionate, skilled individuals who could function as a team and take on the responsibility for growing the church.

The Change in Skillset

Moving through TP2 requires, at minimum, the following changes or additions to the pastor's skillset:

- Takes TP1 skills to the next level
- Hires and fires staff
- Manages program staff
- Sets clear expectations for staff
- Holds staff accountable for expectations

Let's take a closer look at these skills.

Takes TP1 Skills to the Next Level

The journey from two hundred to five hundred is fraught with second-guesses, forks in the road, greener grass, and every other metaphor that invites the pastor to stop kingdom building and start playing church. There are inviting temptations and pressures to refocus the pastor's time and resources on the membership. At this size church, the "What about us?" chorus can seem mighty loud. When a pastor succumbs to these cries, the growth-killing monster "Poor Hiring Choices" rears its head and the church staff roster quickly becomes an age-graded chaplaincy menu. This is why it's more important than ever for the lead pastor to master each of the TP1 skills.

Vision Casting

It's easy for a congregation to lose its vision for the kingdom at this size. Surely we've worked hard enough and grown the church big enough to enjoy some perks such as hiring a youth director and a congregational visitation pastor. Some will call for an "associate minister" who can pick up the lead pastor's slack, such as member visitation, seniors' ministries, and so on. In the face of these demands the lead pastor must be able to effectively and convincingly keep the mission and kingdom vision foremost in the congregation's mind. To put it rather bluntly, if a lead pastor can't cast the vision well enough to keep the church from shooting itself in the foot, it's probably time to take a step back to a TP1 church to relearn the skill.

Ministry Hand-Off

It's more important than ever for the lead pastor to devote the majority of their time and resources to the Invite core process. Although they won't be able to give 70 to 80 percent of their time to inviting, it's important to spend 40 to 50 percent in the presence of the unchurched and connecting new guests to the congregation's ministries. To do this, however, it becomes increasingly important to hand off ministries to others. As the lead pastor moves through TP2 there will be more staff to handle this, but the role of unpaid leaders exponentially increases through this transition, and handing off ministry to these folks is necessary.

Hires and Fires Staff

Although learning to hire and fire begins in TP1, before a pastor completes TP2 they must become proficient at the process. Hiring and firing staff isn't offered as a seminary course, and since many pastors enter full-time ministry because they have a high mercy gift and a love for doing ministry, hiring and firing staff isn't one of their natural skills either. Indeed, the higher the mercy gift, the more difficult it will be for the pastor to hold people accountable, much less to fire them. But unless this skill is mastered, the church will suffer and never reach its potential.

When we consult with churches, one of the chief problems we run into is church polity—or policy—that requires a committee to do the hiring and firing. This practice is devastating to the growth of people, the church, and the kingdom. Few people who sit on personnel committees have enough knowledge about what goes on in the life of a staff person to make a judgment call on their effectiveness. And when a committee hires and fires, triangulation is right around the corner. If a staff person doesn't like a decision made by the lead pastor, that person can go around the lead pastor to the committee.

Here's an example of how devastating personnel-by-committee can be. I (BTB) consulted with a large church with a large staff. The church had grown consistently over the years, but had come to an abrupt plateau a couple years after the current pastor had arrived. It took some investigation, but it turned out that the cessation of growth coincided with a personnel issue. The pastor noted that a particular staff member had been sowing serious discord within the church. After several attempts to rein in the issue, the pastor fired the staff member. However, instead of staying fired, the staff member went to the personnel committee and bargained for their job. Without consulting the pastor, the committee reinstated the staff member and informed the pastor of their decision. From that point on, the pastor's ability to lead and manage staff, and thus to lead the church, was severed. And although the pastor tried to salvage the situation, the church wasn't able to move forward. Ultimately the pastor had to leave and the dysfunctional personnel system had to be dismantled.

An Alternative Hiring–Firing Practice

We realize that most of our readers must deal with existing polity or policies about hiring and firing, and that it can be difficult to dismantle these systems (even though these systems are hurting your church). Over the years I've (BTB) developed a "compromise" practice that allows the personnel committee to play a key part in the process without compromising the lead pastor's hiring and firing abilities.

To begin with, we have to make the following recommendation—as unpopular as we know it will be. For confessional churches with an ordained hierarchy (such as the UMC and PCUSA) we recommend not "calling" any more ordained staff members beyond the lead pastor than are absolutely necessary. The reason for this is because both the hiring and termination process can be seriously hampered by the judicatory. For instance, I (BE) once had to terminate a called associate. Although I immediately relieved the staff member of their responsibilities and removed them from the church, we were still expected to pay their salary and benefits until the pastor could be reassigned. Removing a "called" staff member can be fraught with difficulties; therefore we recommend "hiring" for all other staff positions whenever possible.

When it comes to hiring staff, the church leadership will need to agree that the ultimate responsibility for hiring and firing is in the hands of the lead pastor. Undermining the pastor cannot be an option . . . ever. However, the personnel committee has the ability to hold the pastor accountable for bad decisions.

Second, the lead pastor is responsible for "finding" the candidate of their choice.[1] This candidate is then recommended to the personnel committee for a simple thumbs-up/thumbs-down secret vote. If the candidate is approved, the lead pastor makes the hire (not the committee). If the candidate is not approved, the committee must explain their reasoning to the pastor and the process is repeated. If the personnel committee consistently turns down the pastor's candidate, it's time for the pastor to move on to another church.

No staff member should be a mission; they should be on a mission.

Terminating a staff member can create churchwide trauma, especially if the staff member has been there long enough to become entrenched within the congregation. With this in mind, if a hiring mistake has been made it is critical that the supervisor recognize this as quickly as possible, preferably within the first ninety days. Remember that the primary responsibility of the lead pastor (or of any ministry supervisor) is to the church, not to an individual. In most churches there isn't enough time or resources to deal with a "project" employee. If a staff member can't do their job, terminate them as quickly as possible.

The terminating process looks like this: if a staff member has been underperforming, there should be a paper trail documenting the issue. Every coaching appointment should include the supervisor's notes with any performance deficiencies noted (see appendix for a coaching/mentoring form). In any event, if a staff member needs to be terminated the lead pastor should take the necessary steps as soon as possible. In most cases, a simple "Covenant of Closure" should be signed before the final check is issued. Once the staff member has been removed, the chair of the personnel committee should be notified as soon as possible so that any damage control measures can be taken.

If the personnel committee has concerns about the termination, their only recourse is to hold the lead pastor accountable in some manner—including termination, if warranted. However, if the committee trusts their leader, then they should trust them to make decisions on behalf of the church. If they don't trust their leader then they should replace their leadership with someone they *can* trust.

Manages Program Staff

One of the key responsibilities of the lead pastor at this level is the management and supervision of program staff. It is always a mistake for any staff member to be accountable to a committee, and at this level they should report directly to the lead pastor. Of course this means that the lead pastor may now have to give significant time to mentoring and coaching, and this responsibility will only increase from here on out. The most difficult staff management task a lead pastor will have to master is learning how to be critical, if not ruthless, in evaluating the staffing needs of the church. Remember, effective churches prioritize staffing the core processes.

Jim inherited a number of staff positions when he arrived. The church had fallen into the trap of hiring for membership needs over kingdom building. A few church families had high school-age children and insisted the church hire a full-time youth director. They reasoned that every big church had a vibrant youth program, and so it seemed like the logical next staffing choice. But once they'd hired Ken as their youth director, some seniors began to complain they were being neglected because no one on staff regularly visited them. So Janet was hired part-time to be the visitation minister. Everyone loved Ken and Janet, and Pastor Jim was happy that he didn't have to tend to those responsibilities anyway—it left him even more time to network with the unchurched.

But eighteen months later, Jim realized the church wasn't growing even though several new families visited every week. And so he called his coach and explained the situation. Jim's coach pinpointed the problem: the Retain Them core process was inadequate. New people were coming to the church, but they weren't making lasting connections with the church's ministries or with members of the congregation. It was time to hire a Connect key leader. But the church couldn't afford to take on another full-time staff member. The coach told Jim that he would have to make some hard decisions about his current staff, but Jim said removing either Ken or Janet would be hard on the church. That's when the coach taught Jim one of the most important lessons Jim would have to learn: when it comes to leading a church, the pastor's first priority is the good of the church. Nothing can get in the way of that precedent.

To effectively manage staff Jim had to learn to separate positions from personalities. The chief staffing need in a church this size is to ensure the Retain Them process is efficient and effective. In other words, once the worship pastor and the children's director are in place, the next staff hire should be the Connect key leader—if Jim planned on leading the church to the next level. This meant he might need to eliminate existing staff positions in order to free up the necessary funding for this new hire. We realize this can be a delicate and difficult decision. However, the difficulty is seriously compounded if Jim mentally and emotionally sees Ken's face every time he considers eliminating the youth position. If the lead pastor is unable to make these kinds of difficult staff management decisions, the future of the church is in jeopardy.

Sets Clear Expectations for Staff

Failure to communicate clear expectations is one of the major faults of those new to the role of lead pastor. Unless the staff know what is expected of them in ways they can measure, they are set up for failure. "Grow your area" or "We want more youth" are not clear expectations. "You need to grow the youth group by 50 percent over the next two years" is a clear and measurable expectation. Clear expectations are generally SMART: Specific, Measurable, Actionable, Realistic, and Time-Driven.

THE MISSING EXPECTATIONS

There are two expectations that are often overlooked in this size church. First, too often staff is hired to *do* ministry. Youth ministers are often hired to "lead the youth group." Visitation ministers are often hired to "do visitation." But as we pointed out earlier, staff members are first and foremost leaders, not doers. For instance, the children's director has no business leading a Sunday school class—unless it's to mentor an apprentice, and even then the involvement should be minimal. The lead pastor must make it clear that leadership multiplication is the core expectation and it is on this the staff member will be held most accountable.

Second, although we've said that the lead pastor is responsible for creating an inviting culture, the staff must carry this genetic code as well. We suggest that every staff member be responsible for bringing ten or more new families into church membership each year. And by *responsible*, we mean networking with the unchurched beyond the walls of the church, making connections, and bringing them into the church. If a staff member isn't able to do this then they aren't modeling the congregation's inviting DNA, and if the staff doesn't model it, the congregation won't practice it. Therefore, we recommend setting realistic but specific expectations for each staff member each and every year.

Holds Staff Accountable for Expectations

Hiring the right people is just the beginning of the process of supervising and coaching people into becoming all they can become. Once on board, the responsibility for their growth resides both on them and the lead pastor.

After hiring staff, the lead pastor must:

- Communicate the skills, time applications, and work values involved in the position. And when a person isn't performing adequately, it's the role of the pastor to help them understand what they need to do to perform to the expectations.
- Monitor their progress, especially during the first ninety days following the hire. This means being accessible to the new staff person as well as asking them to provide regular progress reports. Our experience has been if a new staff person hasn't figured out how to achieve the expectations within ninety days, the odds are they never will.
- Provide feedback on how well they are performing their responsibilities. The supervisor needs to provide specific feedback:

"In order to move forward you need to acquire X skill, adopt Y value, and focus more of your time on Z." Unless they know they are underperforming, it is unlikely they will improve. Conversely, staff should also be recognized when they exceed expectations.

Providing Effective Feedback

There's only one thing worse than a broken feedback loop, and that's no feedback loop at all—a practice we find endemic in far too many churches. Effective feedback not only motivates staff to succeed, but it enhances the supervisor's skills as well. Therefore, two-way feedback is important in mentoring staff. Staff members need to have a clear idea of how well they are carrying out their supervisor's expectations, and the supervisor needs to know if they are setting clear expectations and providing the resources needed for each staff person to get their job done.

Although there should be an open feedback loop that is tapped almost daily between the pastor and their closest staff, a slightly more formal assessment is needed at least quarterly. We suggest keeping the assessment quick and simple. For that reason we are not proposing a normal 360 evaluation.[2] A simple two-way form might look like the following:

- Where have I excelled this quarter?
- Where have I missed the mark this quarter?
- What can I do to improve my work next quarter?
- What do you need from me that will make me a better supervisor/staff member?

Be sure to make a copy of the forms and file them in the staff member's personnel file.

It's never wise to keep an underperforming staff member beyond the point you decide they can't do the ministry they were hired to do. The quicker you terminate them, the less turmoil will be caused by their dismissal. In addition, allowing an underperforming staff member to remain sends a negative signal to the rest of the staff. Either they think the pastor doesn't care the person isn't performing or else they decide the pastor isn't aware enough of the situation to remedy it—or worse yet, the pastor doesn't have the guts to do what is necessary, so everyone else has to step up and do extra duty to fill in the gaps. If you've made a bad hire, own up to it and deal with it, even if it's your best friend . . . or it will come back to bite you.

The Change in Values

Jim's coach helped him see that the future of his church, not to mention the kingdom, was through the multiplication of everything. To move through TP2 Jim had to develop a multiplication mindset. Addition was now out of the question. If the church was to continue increasing its impact on the community and the world, it had to learn how to multiply everything: leaders, worship services, locations, and community and world ministries.

The only way to achieve multiplication of everything is by doing ministry through other people. It was imperative for Jim to learn that the only staff members the church could afford were those who could multiply themselves over and over. Two stories illustrate how what we value affects whether or not we develop leaders.

Early on in my (BTB) ministry I led a number of small groups. I measured success by how many people came to these small groups and whether or not the topic *du jour* spawned a lively discussion. Of course, I could only lead a few groups each week, but because I modeled leadership by being the resident scholar it was difficult to find new leaders. Besides, I *enjoyed* being the leader. But in time, I realized it was me who was keeping the church from growing and I had to redefine success. Therefore, when I started new small groups I refused to be the onsite theologian and insisted group members themselves dig for answers as a group. In addition, I surreptitiously apprenticed everyone by delegating leadership responsibilities, including leading prayer and the Bible study. Since it became clear leaders didn't need to have an MDiv or PhD in Bible to lead, I could multiply leaders and small groups in as little as eight weeks. But I didn't count a multiplication as a success unless the leader raised up a new leader and started yet another new small group or ministry.

This second story occurred in the early years of my ministry (BE). I had a staff person who performed excellently during his first year with me. We had grown from nineteen to 250 people in less than eighteen months. Some of the growth came because one particular staff person put in untold hours caring for people. Numerous times he spent all night at the hospital bedside of a member. He valued *doing* ministry to the point that it was impossible for him to develop leaders to do what he was doing . . . after all, he might work himself out of a job. As a result, our growth slowed significantly and three years later we were barely averaging three hundred in worship. I realized that as long as this staff person valued taking care of people rather than transforming them, the church would never reach its potential. This person had to go even though the members and I loved him dearly.

The Change in Time Management

There are two primary shifts in how one spends time at this stage. The most obvious is that the lead pastor spends more time mentoring and coaching his or her staff and even less one-on-one time with members of the congregation. However, the lead pastor must still spend significant time networking with the unchurched to continually fuel and model the invitational mindset.

The second shift is not as obvious, but is perhaps the most critical shift in going to the next level. Jim's coach suggested it was time for Jim to spend time with pastors in churches his size and larger. This meant the church had to allocate additional continuing education money for Jim so he could afford to travel. Jim found that some of his most valuable coaching moments came from conversations with other effective pastors.

Early Signs of Failure to Move through TP2

- Continuing to hold on to all or most of the ministry
- Failing to set clear expectations and to ask for feedback
- Allowing an ineffective staff person to stay on too long

- Being unable to quickly and effectively remove ineffective and non-multiplying staff
- Failing to adopt a multiplication mindset

Just because you've become the pastor of a "big" church doesn't mean there isn't more to learn. As his church continued to grow, Jim began feeling its full weight on his shoulders. The next transition point would be critical for Jim and for the future of the church.

14

The Journey through Transition Point Three

Jim had come a long way on his leadership journey. He had successfully navigated through some of the most turbulent leadership shifts a person can make when leading a church. Although he still had to contend with his mercy gift now and then, he'd learned well how to keep the good of the church in front of him, and as a result the congregation grew. Not only were there more people coming to worship, he could also see the fruit of multiplication everywhere he looked. There were more leaders, more ministries, and more mission opportunities. But something bothered him. Jim was beginning to feel increasingly disconnected from the church's ministries and the church leaders themselves. There were so many ministries going on he found it impossible to remember even the ministry leaders' names. And so Jim turned once again to his coach.

Jim's coach assured him that what he was feeling was normal, and was a signal he had entered TP3. It would be crucial for Jim to learn how to lead effectively through the eyes, hands, and feet of others—and to take his satisfaction from *their* success. His coach called this "leading once removed," and said it applied to everything he did at the church. Jim could no longer spend the time he had networking with the unchurched; others would have to carry this mantle. He would no longer be able to nurture personal relationships with the congregation; he would have to learn to use the power of the pulpit to accomplish that. And he could no longer be responsible for supervising the program staff. He would have to lead through his four key leaders. And Jim's coach said that was only the beginning.

The Change in Skillset

Moving through TP3 requires developing a new reference for "doing" ministry. This can be a difficult shift for hands-on, results-oriented leaders who must now fuel their motivation by experiencing transformation from a distance. To move through TP3, the lead pastor:

- Releases all ministry
- Leads once removed
- Becomes a capable strategist
- Asks the right questions
- May choose to lead through an executive pastor

Let's examine these changes more closely.

Releases All Ministry

Jim's coach made it clear: if Jim was to successfully navigate TP3 he had to free himself of *all* hands-on ministry. The only exception to this would be when he was specifically mentoring or training someone to do that ministry, but even then such actions would be limited.

To make it through this transition point, the lead pastor must be totally disengaged from day-to-day ministry and focused instead on two or three major, mission-critical directives for the entire church. The lead pastor can no longer be concerned about the individual ministries of the church, nor get bogged down in day-to-day decision making. The lead pastor must focus on the whole, asking just one question: "Are our systems in place and working to develop the leaders of the future?"

Leads Once Removed

At this leadership level, the lead pastor simply doesn't have the time or the resources to have a personal relationship with all of the church leaders, let alone every member of the congregation. Therefore it's critical that the lead pastor learn to effectively lead the whole church "once removed."

SUPERVISES ONLY THE FOUR KEY LEADERS

Because of the increasing number of staff, it is necessary for the lead pastor to lean heavily on the key leaders who lead the four core processes. Since they report directly to him, they become the pastor's "go-to" staff. Jim's coach helped him see the wisdom of giving these four staff direct access to him at any time. Because the church is too large for any one person to know everything taking place, the combined knowledge of these four staff becomes the eyes and ears of the lead pastor. Therefore the ability to have absolute trust in these four is crucial.

APPROPRIATES THE POWER OF THE PULPIT

At this size, the lead pastor will never be able to call everyone in the congregation by name. But here's a little secret—the lead pastor can still have a personal relationship with every person in the congregation through the power of the pulpit. Every effective large church pastor has stories of receiving "love letters" from total strangers telling them how they had changed their life. I (BE) still remember the first time I received a note from a perfect stranger telling me that I had actually saved him from committing suicide. Over the last few years of pastoral ministry I have received several such notes. The more never-churched people you reach, the more of these kinds of love notes you will receive.

Never underestimate the power of the pulpit—even if you don't have one!

At this size your relationship with most of the congregation will be at the weekend services when you teach/preach. Never underestimate the power of having the same audience over and over again. What you teach on Sunday is a powerful tool of relationship and multiplication.

125

Becomes a Capable Strategist

At this juncture the lead pastor can never be fixated on the present. Instead their eyes should be on what is needed for the church to continue its multiplication of ministries. Enough is never enough when it comes to increasing the kingdom. Long-term vision comes from reading and analyzing the signs of the times. It's not unusual at this level for a pastor to read twelve or more books a month and share what is learned with the staff. It also means spending the time to see what other churches twice their size are doing.

But it's not enough for the lead pastor to have lots of good ideas. In fact, there's more to effectively leading the church into the future than just setting goals. At this juncture the lead pastor has to consider what strategies will best achieve the vision and the goals that have been put before them. Of course the lead pastor doesn't do this in a vacuum, but with the supportive encouragement of the key leaders, who offer insights. But once a strategy has been chosen, the pastor will need to release it to those who can develop effective tactics and those who have a gift for logistics. Then, when the planning is done, the lead pastor will need to take up the mantle of the vision, strategies, and tactics in order to rally the congregation into action.

Asks the Right Questions

Lead pastors must have plenty of "no agenda time" so they can think and daydream about the future. When someone is overworked, they seldom ask the right questions.

Here are some of the right questions to ask:

- Am I listening to God and allowing the Holy Spirit to guide me when making decisions?
- Is my family happy? Am I happy and fulfilled?
- Is our worship indigenous to the present generation, and what will we have to do to make it indigenous to the next generation?
- Do we have all the systems in place to take us to the next level?
- Is the staff innovative enough, or are they becoming stale?

- Have I given the four key leaders clear expectations, and am I offering regular feedback? Are they doing the same with the staff they supervise?
- Do we have enough staff?
- Do the four key leaders feel comfortable enough to tell me the bad news?
- Do we have enough parking? If not, how do we acquire more, or add another site, or plant another church, or go multi-site?
- Do I know enough about what is going on to feel comfortable staying out of the mix?
- Is all the staff productive, happy, and effective?
- How many adult baptisms are we having?
- Am I measuring the right things?

Chooses to Add an Executive Pastor

When a church approaches one thousand in worship, the lead pastor may want to begin seeking to share the administrative responsibilities with someone with a like mind. This is not a step to take lightly, and many lead pastors opt to wait until the church is significantly larger before investing in this position.

As Jim built relationships with pastors of larger churches, virtually every conversation he had included their confession on how much they relied on their executive pastor. The more Jim talked with them, the more he realized the need to redo his staff configuration one more time.

After a lengthy search, Jim hired an executive pastor. But before he did, he had another conversation with his coach, who told him the most important part of hiring an executive pastor was finding someone who shared his DNA and vision for the church. Otherwise, the hire would be disastrous for Jim and for the future of the congregation. The key question Jim should ask of any executive pastor candidate was, "Would I like to spend a month isolated on a desert island with this person?"

The shift to an executive pastor is a huge step that can be either productive or destructive. It requires a healthy ego on the part of the lead pastor, because now not only are they not involved in any hands-on ministries, but the lead pastor may no longer be the coach of the four key leaders. This is why the executive pastor must have the same DNA as the lead pastor. There can be absolutely no variance in how they understand the mission of the church. Jim was at a crucial moment in the life of the church. A misstep here could derail everyone's hard work.

With the addition of an executive pastor, the lead pastor must learn how to lead through them. Instead of having direct accountability, the lead pastor sets expectations through the executive pastor—even for the four key leaders. This is where things can easily get out of control if the lead pastor doesn't spend enough time with the executive pastor to ensure they are both on the same page. If the two don't share the same DNA, a train wreck is inevitable. We suggest the lead pastor meet with the executive pastor *at least* weekly to specifically discuss the vision of the church and how the staff is accomplishing that vision.

The Change in Values

At this stage the lead pastor must value the importance of living out ministry through others, including through the executive pastor, and trusting that person with the care and feeding of the staff. This is perhaps the second most difficult shift in work values a pastor will ever make.

Our experience has taught us that most creative lead pastors love to cast vision and set the direction for the church, but seldom like to follow through with the implementation of the details. This is where the executive pastor enters the picture.

A good way to make the distinction between the lead pastor and the executive pastor is by examining Warren Bennis's famous saying, "Managers are people who do things right and leaders are people who do the right thing."[1] The lead pastor focuses on making sure the right things are done, guides the overall direction, and sets the course for the entire church, whereas the executive pastor makes sure ministry is done right. One leads and one manages. The lead pastor makes sure the right things are done, and the executive pastor makes sure they are done right. There is a huge difference between the two.

The issue here is not either/or, but where the person puts the emphasis and what skillset they bring to the table. A great lead pastor has the ability to see the church's direction from a 10,000-mile-high view and can then effectively cast that vision. A great executive pastor catches the vision, analyzes it through a magnifying glass, organizes it, and makes it a reality by breathing life into the details.

The Change in Time Management

This change is obvious. The lead pastor devotes most of their time to three things:

1. Spending time on their spiritual development. At this point, so many people depend on the spiritual leadership of the lead pastor and so many eyes are watching that any moral failure will cause ripple effects far beyond the local congregation. The magnitude of such responsibility usually weighs heavily on a lead pastor, who cares deeply about their flock. A pastor at this size church needs a large dose of free time to refresh. It is not unusual at this point for a pastor to spend 50 percent of their time developing their spiritual life.

2. Spending time with the four key leaders, and eventually shifting that to time with the executive pastor. The only way these two pastors become one in their hopes and dreams is by hanging out together . . . a lot.

3. Spending time preparing the message to be delivered every week. Perhaps it is important to say that at this point the average pastor in a megachurch preaches/teaches some thirty-five to thirty-seven times a year, with the executive pastor preaching/ teaching the other weeks. Very few people are capable of delivering a riveting message fifty-two times a year. And those pastors who try are clearly not taking care of themselves spiritually or intellectually. Successful lead pastors at this level take their time off, and they continue to check out the churches at the "next level."

Best Practices of the Executive Pastor

Frankly, a whole book could be written on the role and responsibilities of an executive pastor. The truth is, though, that they are all negotiated within the relationship between lead and executive pastor. For instance, the way Glen Kreun at Saddleback handled his responsibilities was significantly different from the ways of Dan Shima at New Hope, Oahu. However, there *are* some common practices executive pastors share. The effective executive pastor:

- Is a strategic thinking partner who is loyal to the senior pastor, the executive team, and the church's mission and brand
- Models healthy accountability to the congregation by being accountable to the lead pastor
- Does everything possible to build, develop, strengthen, and maintain complete trust with the lead pastor, governing board, other staff members, and the congregation
- Is willing to ask the hard questions
- Is able to infuse the lead pastor's DNA into the team in order to fulfill the mission
- Interprets and organizes the lead pastor's vision for the key leaders and ensures its implementation
- Hires, fires, and supervises the key leaders
- Functions in a way that ensures the entire staff moves as one
- Handles staff with grace more than by law, and yet holds them accountable to high expectations
- Helps staff understand how what they do fits into the vision and mission of the church
- Ensures a continual high level of integrity and dependability with a strong sense of results-orientation

Frankly, the executive pastor is the lead pastor's right hand, confidant, co-worker, friend, and at times maybe even family. Be very careful who you hire; in terms of the kingdom, your choice is at least as important as the one you made (or may yet make) for your life-partner.

Early Signs of Failure to Move through TP3

- Failure to release control of the tactics and logistics in vision achievement
- Failure to be satisfied with achieving ministry and mission through the leadership of others
- Failure to hire and/or spend significant time with the four key leaders at the front of this transition
- Failure to hire and/or spend significant time with the executive pastor during this transition
- Failure to spend enough time developing own spiritual life
- Failure to continually become a more effective communicator

---

At some time in the life of every large church, the leadership is faced with a dilemma: Can it afford to grow? In the next chapter Jim is faced with this question and is forced to navigate the final transition point.

15

The Journey through Transition Point Four

Jim had come a long way in his personal growth. Having maneu-
vered through three gut-wrenching shifts in church leadership, he
had now arrived—or so he thought.

Not long after he hired the executive pastor, the two of them were
having a conversation about the future of the church. During their
conversation it became obvious that the church had become about
as big as it could become in the space it had. If the church was going
to continue to grow, it would have to have more parking and more
space for worship. They were approaching 75 percent capacity in all
areas of ministry and knew the time to act was upon them. Jim and
the executive pastor spent hours in prayer about how to proceed. It
simply wasn't in their genes to hang out a "No Vacancy" sign.

Again Jim turned to his coach, who helped him understand that
from now on space issues would always be one of the major challenges
to reaching more people for the kingdom. One of his prime objectives
would become staying ahead of the space issues.

Because Jim had been visiting with other pastors and reading many
books about innovative churches, he knew there were more options
than the traditional ones of relocating the church or purchasing

contiguous property. Finally, he decided it was time to explore becoming a multi-site congregation.

The first thing Jim's coach helped him to see was that shepherding a church in more than one location is more complicated than shepherding in just one location. Not only would he have to lead once removed, he would have to lead from a physical distance as well. Many pastors make the assumption that if you can run a single location church well you can just as easily run multiple locations. Not so . . . not even close.

Becoming a multi-site church is like having twins. If you've ever had twins you know that one plus one equals more than two. It's not just adding another site—it's multiplying locations. Geography makes everything more complex, especially for the staff. Even they have to learn to coach and delegate from a distance. In other words, not only does the lead pastor have to traverse this transition point, but so does the staff. Making this decision means the staff has to make a gigantic shift in their leadership—and it's likely that some staff members won't be able to navigate the transition and will need to be replaced. This is not a transition to be considered lightly, and yet it's a transition that more and more church leaders are facing.

We're aware that not all churches will choose to become multi-site. However, we wish every effective church would, because we believe multi-site is the most cost-effective and productive way to solve a church's space issues without uprooting the congregation. So we're focusing this chapter on moving through TP4 by becoming a multi-site church. Later in this chapter we will discuss some of the space issues churches face if they choose not to become multi-site.

However, we hope the day comes when most multi-site campuses will happen because they are part of a strategy instead of a reaction to a space problem. It's our opinion that by 2050 multiple-site churches will be the norm for growing churches. The need for one-site locations will no longer be an issue.

The Change in Skillset

- Provides deep, profound teaching
- Mentors/coaches campus pastors

- Thinks and acts glocally
- Ensures that back door systems are in place
- Focuses on the future
- Focuses on adequate space

Let's look at each of these.

Provides Deep, Profound Teaching

Good teaching has always been important to the growth of the church and the kingdom, but at this stage it becomes the primary tool of the lead pastor. As such, the quality and relevance of every message has to consistently be top drawer. There's no longer the option of a bad message . . . ever. It's not unusual at this stage for the pastor to secure someone to help with the research for the message. Nor is it unusual for the pastor to spend as much time on teaching as on visioning for the future.

But it's not just the content of the sermon that must be top drawer. At this level of preaching, the lead pastor may spend more hours rehearsing the delivery than researching and writing the sermon combined. The days of extemporaneous comments are pretty much over at this point, and yet the delivery must feel extemporaneous, personal, warm, and relaxed as well.

Mentors/Coaches Campus Pastors

Now Jim is the coach of the coaches, and while the coaching skill-set remains the same, it is complicated by the fact that those being coached are not always nearby. If the campus pastor is local then there should be some cross-pollination during staff meetings. However, if the other site or sites are not local then the issues may be complicated by feelings of isolation. At a minimum, regular video conferencing is in order. Any way you cut it, putting geographical distance between the lead pastor and campus pastor creates additional challenges.

We've been doing a lot of long-distance coaching over the last few years, and we've discovered it's effective to ask far more questions than you would if you were coaching on-site. Asking more questions requires more supervisory time to accomplish the same level of success as when geography isn't a factor.

Thinks and Acts Glocally

Churches this size need to think and act glocally, especially if they are going to become multi-site. *Glocal* means the church has the capacity to think beyond the border of their city, state, or nation, as well as focus on their own backyard. The lead pastor must seek God's wisdom on how to take the church beyond the church's current ministry area, whether that means becoming multi-site, planting a church, developing a digital ministry, or developing an overseas ministry. Our experiences confirm that the more a church focuses on sending its people to serve in foreign fields, the more likely it is the church will be developing backyard missionaries.

Thinking glocally also means that location is no longer an issue. All of the church's locations are considered equal in their importance, whether local or foreign.

When a church reaches this point in its growth it has the capacity for influence far beyond that of the average church because of its resources and experience. And it is the role of the lead pastor to focus the church as far beyond itself as the resources allow. And remember, "To whom much has been given, the more that is required" (see Luke 12:48).

Ensures That Back Door Systems Are in Place

Earlier we talked about the six systems every church needs in order to be effective. We now need to look at two of these more closely, because at this point in the journey systems become a critical component of effective apprenticing, and multiplying leaders is the heart and soul of the effective church.

The six systems of the leadership development process are: (1) identifying, (2) enlisting, (3) equipping, (4) deploying, (5) coaching, and (6) celebration. In churches under one thousand in worship, deploying, coaching, and celebration are the most important systems to have in place. The church is small enough to be able to identify most of the newcomers. But in a church larger than this, the most difficult aspects of leadership are identifying and enlisting. These are the systems that close the back door.

Now we get to the elephant in the room of most large churches: the *big* back door. Few large churches have an effective system for closing the back door, and fewer still have staff specifically deployed to close the back door. It's not unusual for a large church to take in several hundred new members each year and yet not see an increase in their average worship attendance. Guests come, they like what they see, and they may even join, but they end up getting lost between the cracks of the retaining process and are never seen again. We've even joked that the best place to plant a church is across the street from a megachurch. The exodus through their back door alone will grow the new church.

But the fact is, it is far easier to keep people than to attract new people. Therefore, no matter how large a church becomes, it must have an intentional strategy for connecting with *all* of the people who sign in. Most large churches use the excuse that there are simply too many people to connect with all of them. To that we say: shame on you.

The sheer number of people requires large churches to have these two systems, identifying and enlisting, firmly in place and every staff member working those systems to close the back door. Consider a church of fifteen hundred in worship. During any given month three thousand different people come through the doors. Often up to one quarter of these are first-time visitors. It's easy now for people to come and go without ever being noticed. On top of that, large churches require large numbers of servants to make the ministry happen. So it's imperative a church growing beyond one thousand sets some systems in place that: (1) identify new people and potential leaders; (2) enlist people into a small group, ministry, or leadership position; (3) equip people to move up the leadership chain; (4) deploy people into actual ministry; (5) coach them along the way; and (6) celebrate their achievements. It doesn't really matter what these systems look like as long as every leader in the church understands how these systems function and how to work them.

When developing systems it's a matter of becoming so intentional that no one gets overlooked. Therefore, in a large church it's critical to build in redundant and overlapping systems so that if someone falls through one crack, there's a safety net to catch them and a friendly hand to help them find the next step in their connection journey. Imagine what the kingdom would be like if even half of those people bleeding out the back door of these large churches were instead connected, discipled, and deployed as backyard missionaries.

Now do you see why these two systems are so important, and why the lead pastor has to ensure they are in place? It's one thing to have the Connect core process staffed. It's another to have a system in place that allows the church to identify and then recruit dozens of first-time people each week.

So what does your church do to close the back door? It really doesn't matter what this system looks like. We've given you several options in previous chapters. All that matters is that you have a system in place, and that it works. The wise lead pastor knows the back door is the weakest link in a church this size and focuses attention on closing it.

Focuses on the Future

One of the reasons we are so adamant on the pastor having regular downtime to scratch their head is because at this transition, the lead pastor's heart and mind has to be in the future, not the present. It is usually the case that most staff are so engrossed in their ministry that they are focused mostly on the present issues that must be addressed in order to continue to reach and apprentice new people. So, one of the universal skills of a lead pastor at this level is to be able to intuitively see into the future. By this we mean to anticipate what might be the next challenge or barrier to the growth of the kingdom.

One of the things that separates the good from the great leaders is the ability to see a looming crisis and turn it into an opportunity.

Focuses on Adequate Space

It is impossible to over-stress the importance of understanding and responding to the ever-present space challenges of the church as it grows beyond one thousand in worship. From this point on space issues just get worse . . . or, we should say, more challenging. They never abate, not as long as you continue to reach more people. So the lead pastor must ensure that the church and staff are always at least two years ahead of the 80 percent capacity rule or the church is likely to lose momentum. It's always harder to regain momentum than it is to sustain it.

If you think parking and seating are the only capacity issues you may have to face, think again. Here are the most critical space issues that, if not addressed, will cause a church to plateau:

- Parking is often the first bottleneck. Church architects too often get this one wrong. If your church parking lot was designed by an architect who designs mall parking lots, the church would have an off-street parking space for every 1.75 people on the premise at the prime hour and the prime season. In other words, a space for every 1.75 people on Easter.

- The larger the church becomes, the more likely entrance and exit issues become problematic. Churches beyond one thousand in worship must have more than one "front door." A good rule of thumb is two major entrances/exits for every fifteen hundred in worship.

- The number of people who can comfortably sit in worship is always critical. Although the standard is twenty-four inches of seating space per person, that pretty much only works if everyone chooses to stand (or sit) in a mosh-pit environment. At 80 percent, the worship center is at capacity. At 70 percent, you'd better be scrambling for alternatives.

- The church lobby is next in line when it comes to space that stifles growth. Today's lobby is more than the mouth of a funnel that gets people in or out of the building. In most churches it's the primary socializing and connecting space. Scrimp here and you'll find it increasingly difficult to stem the flow through your back door. The rule of thumb for capacity keeps getting larger and larger. We used to recommend that the lobby should be one-third the size of the worship center. Now that figure is closer to half.

- The nursery contributes its own share of problems. Consider Willow Creek's challenge of changing over two thousand diapers on an average Sunday morning. Talk about needing a system! The nursery has become one of the most important rooms in the church because: (1) parents today are having fewer children, (2) parents are waiting longer to have children, (3) parents carry a lot of guilt about leaving their children in the care of other people for so many hours of the week, (4) noncustodial parents have been known to kidnap children from institutions, including churches, and (5) children are accustomed to having quality care at daycare centers during the week. A rule of thumb here is thirty square feet per child.

- Next come the hallways. The width of hallways today is nearly double what it was in the 1950s. Although you will need to check local code, a good rule of thumb is ten feet wide.

- One more fact about space issues: the more worship venues you have, the more likely your church is to grow. Whether or not you go multi-site, you still have to expand the number of opportunities for worship. And the best way to stifle growth, if you do choose to relocate or purchase adjacent property, is to reduce the number of worship services just because more worship space becomes available. It's much easier to break three thousand in worship with four services half-full than with two full services. In other words, if you have the time or alternative space to start multiple services rather than increasing your square footage, you're more likely to see fruit from those headaches—at a lot lower cost.

Certainly there are additional capacity issues that the lead pastor will need to consider, but these are the ones that regularly stunt the church's growth.

The Change in Values

The most difficult transition for Jim and the staff when they went multi-site was learning to value the success of all locations equally. They could not talk about the "main campus." For a multi-site church to be effective, every location must essentially be equal in every aspect of ministry. If there's even a whiff that the "satellite" sites are somehow inferior, the congregation and staff may become resentful, and it becomes increasingly difficult to maintain the core DNA across all campuses. Maintaining equality is not as easy as it sounds, but that is what you *must* do if you want each of the sites to thrive. This concept must be communicated throughout the church, including the church's website.

One of the best ways we've seen to glue multi-site churches together is the use of Community Christian Church's Big Idea.[1] All of the sites use the same message, theme, and graphics as the original site. This ensures the DNA is continually pumped into all locations.

Whether or not a church chooses to go multi-site, if the lead pastor hasn't learned to totally rely on staff to function with little to no supervision by this time, the odds of the church continuing to grow are next to nil. As we said earlier, one of the huge staff changes that must occur before breaking the one thousand mark is the ability of your staff to cease being players and begin functioning as coaches. We have also said it's the lead pastor's responsibility to give general direction to the church, but at this size the implementation of that direction has to be handed off to well-empowered staff members who are self-starters. Any form of micromanaging curtails staff productivity.

Excellence in all things must become one of the lead pastor's core values at this level. This is especially true in both the worship and children's ministries. The lead pastor must be continually raising quality expectations, not only of the staff, but of every leader who puts their hand and heart into ministry. What people expect in a church of one thousand doesn't cut it in a church twice that size.

Excellence in Worship

When it comes to worship, the lead pastor needs to remind the staff that we are living in an *experience economy* that is not going away. Today, if it doesn't first entertain, stimulate, and touch all of the senses, then it won't educate or be the kind of worship that connects spirit to the Spirit. Church leaders will have to get over their bias against entertainment if they want to communicate the gospel. Of course, the opposite is true: entertainment without the gospel is meaningless.

Children's Ministry

When it comes to children's ministry, the word "edutainment" is already the name of a popular catalog that targets educators. Sesame Street began the trend in 1969 when it launched a truly revolutionary method of combining education and entertainment. The trend in children's education continues to become increasingly entertaining as networks marry television programming to children's internet gaming. Did you know that 80 percent of children under age five are adept at using the internet?[2] No longer are children willing to come to Sunday school, sit at a table, and listen to a teacher read a lesson.[3]

The Change in Time Management

At this point the lead pastor either takes on the responsibility of coaching the campus pastors or assigns this responsibility to someone *other than* the executive pastor. The executive pastor assumes more of a direct role in helping relieve the stress that multi-sites create for the staff at the original location.

Key Questions to Ask

- Have I forgotten our original passion for mission?
- Have I allowed innovation to take a backseat to excellence?
- Have any of the four core leaders become distracted?
- Does it take most of our resources to feed the institution?
- Has our dependence on God been replaced by self-sufficiency?[4]

As you can see, growing a church is no different than growing leaders, because the church is nothing more than people on a journey to be more Christlike. In all the talk about growing the church, we should never forget that the church is *people* and is the sign of God's kingdom here on earth. Our goal is never to grow a large church; our goal is to enfold as many people as possible into the kingdom. The growth of the church is simply a byproduct.

Now it's time to take a look at some of the basics that apply to all staff.

16

Staffing Basics

Once a church passes one hundred in worship, staffing begins to take center stage. As a church passes through five hundred in worship, staff is as important as the lead pastor. And when a church passes one thousand in worship, every staff person must assume full responsibility for the multiplication of leaders and ministry as well as the growth of the church. Therefore, we need to spend some time on staff basics.

It's All in Your Paradigm

Everything a person invests their time, energy, and money into is determined by their ministry paradigm.

Two huge paradigms separate effective staff from ineffective staff. The actions of ineffective staff are determined by a paradigm that tells them, "Our role is to take care of people and to do ministry." The actions of effective staff are determined by a paradigm that tells them, "Our role is to transform people." The staff's effectiveness depends on which paradigm fills their hearts.

The paradox of these two paradigms is that you can take care of people without transforming them—but you can't transform people

Leadership Journey for Staff

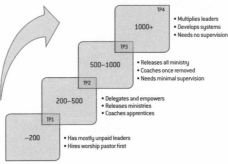

TP4 1000+	• Multiplies leaders • Develops systems • Needs no supervision
TP3 500–1000	• Releases all ministry • Coaches once removed • Needs minimal supervision
TP2 200–500	• Delegates and empowers • Releases ministries • Coaches apprentices
TP1 –200	• Has mostly unpaid leaders • Hires worship pastor first

without first caring for them. We've suggested this before, but it bears repeating. Effective staff members make sure both sides of the paradigm are operative, whereas ineffective staff members remain focused only on taking care of people. Tell us your paradigm and we'll tell you whether your church is effective and growing.

Hiring Staff

There's no doubt about it: hiring staff is one of the most risky practices in the church today. Hire the wrong person and you may find yourself doing battle with the Furies as the congregation spins out of control. But hire the right person and the church will see the kind of growth, on multiple levels, that you could only dream of.

Two paradigms say it all:
Do you take care
of people?
Do you transform
people?

Of course, the most effective and efficient way of finding the right candidate is to be intentional in your mentoring and multiplication processes. If you've been apprenticing someone for a year, you already know whether or not they have the church's DNA deeply embedded in their soul. You know if they produce measurable fruit. And you have a pretty good idea whether or not they fit your staff's ethos. However, it's still important to do due diligence when considering even a long-time apprentice; therefore, we recommend engaging at least some of the same steps you would take if you were hiring someone from outside the congregation.

Tips for Hiring a Team Player

You can hire the top candidate who has all the right qualifications—and still find yourself in a world of hurt. I (BTB) hired what looked and interviewed like a great candidate as a worship pastor only to have her stage a coup for my job. Although I'd interviewed the candidate as well as I knew how, there were clearly some gaps in what I was looking for. The maxim for all hires is: "Hire for passion; train for skills." That will serve you well for most positions. But when it comes to the lead pastor's core team and for other significant positions, there are a number of other criteria that should be used whenever you're looking for a team member. The following qualities are ones I developed over the years, and they're listed in order of importance.

1. **Passion.** When I shared the mission and vision (and the rest of the DNA) of the church, if their eyes weren't afire, they were a miss.
2. **Loyalty.** After the coup attempt, I learned to never hire anyone I didn't think was going to be 100 percent loyal to me. They didn't have to agree with me all the time, but if they disagreed they would do so in my office one-on-one, and *nowhere* else. This was one of two areas where I developed a no-tolerance policy (the other is breaches of ministerial ethics).
3. **Teachability.** I only hired those who knew they didn't know it all and were hungry to learn more and flexible enough to suspend their judgment long enough to give something new an honest try.
4. **Chemistry.** If we didn't click, it was an immediate nix.
5. **Teamwork.** Did they have a history of playing nice on the playground, and could they gather enough friends for a good game of kickball? If not, they weren't going to do well on our team.

6. **Intuition.** Mine. If I had any nagging doubts or red flags, I'd keep looking. I would reconsider if the "right" person didn't come along, but if my intuition hiccupped, I'd take note.

7. **Intuition.** My wife's. If her spirit said no, that was good enough for me, without question. I've been burned too many times from not listening to her heart. She has an incredible gift of discernment and I pay heed to it. Find someone who has that kind of intuition, if yours isn't incredible.

8. **Effectiveness.** I always wanted to know what the person had grown before. Whether they were from within or outside our church, I didn't hire anyone who hadn't shown the ability to grow whatever they were responsible for.

9. **Ability.** Notice this is dead last. If everything else checked out but they didn't have all the skills they were going to need, I considered them anyway. If they scored well in everything else I would hire them, and we'd get them trained at our expense.

Keep these things in mind when you hire, and you won't go too far wrong.

Hiring from Outside the Church

We touched on hiring earlier, and you can find much more information on hiring in *Unfreezing Moves*.[1] We're not going to repeat everything here. However, the following process will give you an idea of the extent of diligence necessary to ensure a good hire.

Most hiring processes begin with a résumé or with "papers" from the denominational office. The problem with depending on either of these is that a résumé is little more than a marketing flier, and denominational papers tend to make most candidates look nearly identical. About the only thing you can count on with these documents is that if you can't actually speak to the references, they're not much good (and if the references won't be forthright, then you might as well shuffle the papers and draw one at random).

Regardless of how you find your first few possibilities, the next hiring steps include extensive phone (or video conference) interviews followed by serious reference and background checking. Once you've narrowed the field, it's time to drill down and really get to know your candidates.

It's been said "The best indicator of future performance is past performance," and it's from these words that the behavioral interview was hatched. Behavioral interviews go well beyond "Tell me about your last position" and "Why are you interested in this job?" kinds of questions. Instead, behavioral interviews press the candidate to reveal their past performance by asking them to provide details of how they accomplished tasks. We recommend questions such as "Tell us about a time when you gathered a group of people for an event" and "Describe a time when you accomplished a task through the hands of others." You might also ask questions such as "Share how you relate to unchurched and non-Christian people. How have you built relationships with them, and what results have you seen?" Most candidates should be able to positively answer any behavioral question you may ask. However, you're not looking for an ordinary staff hire; you're looking for someone with a proven track record. Therefore, you will need to repeat the same question at least one more time, and when possible two or three or more times, depending on how important the behavior is to you. The candidate may not have four specific ministry answers to a particular question, but if they can answer how they've gathered a group of people for a rummage sale, a PTA event, and a local concert, as well as a new Sunday school class, you'll be able to get a sense of their effectiveness.

As you narrow your search, it's a good idea to have them take a personality inventory. I (BE) had potential candidates take a Birkman Personality Profile, which would tell us if they were a fit with our team and give us ideas on how to work with that person if we hired them.[2] The DiSC is another excellent tool that offers similar feedback.

If you like what you see in the candidate, it's time to bring them on-site for interviews with all the lead staff. I (BE) would have them stay in my home so we could simply hang out together for a while. The next day I would spend a couple of hours with them, asking what we consider to be key questions:

- "Describe your spiritual journey for me." If they couldn't excite me with their journey, the interview was over and they would return home.

- "Here is our mission statement—how do you feel about it?" We were looking for something akin to "This is what I've been looking for all my life!"
- "If we hire you, what value would you bring to our mission?" This question was designed to see if they understood our mission and their gifts.

Once a candidate makes it through these questions, the candidate should be interviewed by each of the lead staff. Each staff member should be able to say yes or no. If anyone says no, don't make the hire. When there is unanimity in the staff it ensures the staff's buy-in and makes everyone responsible for the new hire's success.

Finally, if everything looks good, send the candidate home and ask them to write up their job description. If their job description shows they understand the mission and how to achieve it, you can be pretty sure you've made a good decision.

When hiring staff, *nothing* is as important as the heart of the candidate. Skill can be acquired; but a heart for the unchurched can't be taught. You want to hire people with a backyard missionary heart for those who aren't yet in a relationship with Jesus. People who have this heart are worth spending the time needed to build them into the leader God created them to be.

One more thing: always hire for character over skill. We've seen very talented people flame out because of a character flaw, and we've seen talented people provide mediocre results because they treated ministry like a job rather than a passion.

Standards for Judging Staff Performance

One of the main responsibilities of anyone who supervises other staff is evaluating the performance of those they supervise. As we emphasized earlier, one of the key responsibilities of a supervisor is to provide clearly defined expectations. Once that is done, it's important for the supervisor to evaluate performance, give feedback, and decide the value of the person's ministry to the mission of the church.

Here are some guidelines for such an evaluation.

Exceptional Performance

This person:

- Consistently exceeds all ministry requirements
- Continually improves on their skills
- Achieves results in ways that build up and support other staff
- Is given some of the toughest assignments
- Demonstrates the ability to handle more than what's assigned
- Demonstrates leadership ability in all assigned areas
- Always goes beyond what is expected
- Is empowered to do ministry and doesn't need delegation instructions
- Is an ongoing learner
- Values getting ministry done through other people
- Would be hard to replace

Effective Performance

This person:

- Usually meets or exceeds all ministry requirements
- Usually improves in some area of their skillset
- Achieves results in ways that usually build up and support other staff
- Demonstrates leadership potential in most areas assigned
- Always does what is asked of them
- Is empowered to do some aspects of ministry and needs delegation for others
- Is always teachable
- Works hard at getting ministry done through others
- Is considered a valuable staff member but could be replaced

Mediocre Performance

This person:

- Sometimes meets or exceeds all ministry requirements
- Is not at the point where empowerment is possible

- Does not achieve results in ways that build up and support other staff
- Requires significant supervision
- Occasionally demonstrates leadership capability
- Is teachable most of the time
- Does most of the ministry themself
- Would not give the supervisor heartburn if they were no longer on staff

Of course the goal for all staff is exceptional performance, but few achieve such a standard all the time. When it comes to the other two levels of performance, the key question to ask is "Which staff members have the potential to move up to the exceptional level?" The larger the church, the more essential it is that everyone on staff have this potential. As soon as you decide a staff person doesn't have what it takes to move up into the "effective" or "exceptional" levels, help them find a place to serve in another church where their level of skill can be used effectively.

Never let a staff person become a personal project or mission. Instead, they must be *on* a mission. Replace them and move on. Failure to cut your losses as soon as possible always results in hurting the morale of the entire staff and undermining the church's potential.

Things Staff May Never Do

Over the years we've learned that it's important to set a few boundaries that staff should never step across. Here are a few of the most important boundaries to set.

- Staff may never do ministry that someone else could do, unless they are specifically mentoring another person.
- Staff may never do anything that would embarrass the church in any way.
- Staff may never overspend the money allocated to their ministry.
- Staff may never assume that no one else can do their ministry as well as they can.

- Staff may never do anything that would break the trust of the congregation, board, or staff peers.
- Staff may never cause or allow conditions to exist that are unfair, unlawful, or undignified for anyone in the church.
- Staff may never fail to meet a deadline or accomplish a task they agreed to.

Effective Staff Meetings

I (BE) was talking with a young pastor I was mentoring. The subject was how to get her staff to make the shift from being "players" to "equippers." When she asked why it wasn't happening and what she could do about it, I asked, "Tell me, what do you do in your staff meeting?" Looking puzzled, she responded, "We have a devotional and some teaching, do the calendar, and review our past and upcoming programs." Quickly I said, "Well, you get what you measure. You're not measuring people or equipping; you're measuring programs."

If you want your staff to cease being players and become scouts and coaches, it's imperative to put an emphasis on people and equipping in staff meetings. Staff meetings should focus mostly on two aspects of ministry: people and the needs of the community. It's ineffective to focus on programs or perfecting the calendar—this can and should be done via a shared calendar and/or digital information sharing. As we've said, we've found it helpful to talk about staff developing their "To Be" lists rather than their "To Do" lists. "To Be" lists contain the names of people staff members are either mentoring or discipling. Staff that don't have intentional apprentices aren't worth much to an effective church. And we're referring to *all* the staff, including the lead pastor.

To help staff focus more on the community than the church, consider holding the staff meeting in some public place in order to emphasize the importance of what goes on outside the four walls of the church. I (BTB) regularly held staff meetings in local coffee shops, restaurants, the mall, and parks. Being in the community helped my staff keep their vision where it needed to be. On one occasion I took my staff to the top of a hill that overlooked the city we served. While looking over the homes, schools, businesses, and busy highways, we took turns praying for those we were entrusted with, and prayed that our church would bring the tangible touch of Jesus to them. We never saw the city in quite the same way again.

Here are a few typical questions that might be asked during a staff meeting:

- Who have you added this week to your "To Be" list?
- Who have you taken off the list, and why?
- How many new people did you meet this week, and what did you learn that we need to know?
- Who is new in the small group ministry, and how many new apprentices are there this week?
- Have this month's new members found their way into the church?
- What are you doing to improve your spiritual health?
- What new community needs have you discovered this week?
- How many people are you responsible for sending out into the community or world this week?
- How many community projects are we involved in?

Common Staffing Mistakes

Many people have walked the staffing trail ahead of you and have experienced more than one detour. We see no reason to duplicate their mistakes. Every great pastor has made their share of mistakes while learning how to staff, and as you've no doubt discerned, we've made our share of mistakes working with our staffs too. So let's get the superhero stuff out of the way and see staffing for what it is: hard work with a steep learning curve.

The most common mistakes we see pastors making when hiring or terminating staff are:

- Hiring a youth pastor as the first additional staff member instead of a worship leader (most youth pastors are responsible for only a handful of youth). Unfortunately most church leaders still have not gotten the message that the world we live in has *one* universal language: music, and that mostly rock'n'roll. If you look at church plants that do well from the beginning, the vast majority of them have either a paid part-time or full-time worship leader. Today, music is an essential part of the message people hear. Make your first hire a worship leader who loves Jesus and understands today's culture.

- Hiring a person when in doubt because the job needs filling. It's better to do without staff than to hire someone you will have to let go (or wish you could let go) in a short time.

- Putting off terminating someone even though you know you should let them go. Cut your losses as soon as possible. Even unqualified paid servants build relationships within the congregation. The longer they stay, the more relationships they develop, and the more people will get hurt when you let them go.

- Having someone on the staff who *is* a mission rather than being *on* a mission. Many congregations have long-term staff that the church has outgrown who no longer function effectively. They are kept because they're "family." As a result, the mission suffers. The smaller the church, the more likely it is that some long-term, ineffective staff can't be let go due to the chaos it would cause. When this is the case, instead of keeping them as staff move their salary into the mission budget and hire someone to fill their role. Or better yet, give them severance pay and a great retirement party. Do whatever it takes to remove them as quickly as possible. There's no way to do it painlessly, so stop procrastinating and just do it.

- Hiring people based on credentials rather than on their particular character, passion, gifts, and skills. When hiring outside your church, you should always inquire into what that person has built in the past, whether a business, youth ministry, or anything else. When hiring from within, you should have been evaluating their service as a member long before you put them on staff.

- Hiring associate pastors who are generalists instead of hiring specialists. There is room for only one generalist on the staff: the lead pastor.

———

Perhaps by now you're asking the question we get asked so often: "How do you transition staff who function as players into scouts and coaches who multiply themselves?" That is the subject of the next chapter.

17

The Player-Coach Dilemma

Every church we've ever worked with has admitted they need more leaders. As we said earlier, effective leadership is hard to find, and it's even harder to develop. In most churches, especially small and medium ones, staff are more often *doing* ministry rather than leading others in doing ministry.

Recently I (BTB) was consulting at a rather large church. On Sunday morning I discovered the children's pastor teaching Sunday school in a classroom full of four- and five-year-olds. This pastor had not raised up any substitute teachers or apprentice teachers. When I asked her why, she said, "I really enjoyed teaching the four- and five-year-olds."

Although there's nothing wrong with wanting to teach preschoolers, when you're on staff at a large church and your job is leading the children's ministry, your primary job should be leading and coaching adults who work directly with the children. When staff members find themselves involved in *doing* ministries like these, it speaks to their ineffectiveness as a leader. They may be great players, but being a great player does not make anyone a great coach (for instance, Bart Starr and Michael Jordan both come to mind).

Most churches have too few players and even fewer leaders (coaches and scouts). When someone isn't playing and they aren't leading, there's only one place left for them: in the stands (pews) with all the rest of the spectators. Therefore, our *first* task in developing leaders

155

is to help move more of those spectators out of the pews and onto the field as players. Only then can we help them into leadership.

Let's begin by looking at the player-coach matrix.

The Player-Coach Matrix

	Spectator	Player	Coach	Scout
Model	See One	Do One	Teach One	Recruit One
Key	Watching	Practicing	Delegating/ Empowering	Watching
Pitfalls	Disengaged	"My Way"	Micromanaging	Disengaged
Tools	Visioning	Apprenticing	Coaching	Discernment

This matrix provides the outline for each of the following sections. Each column represents the movement from spectator through scout and each row provides a key insight for each position. The first row is a paraphrase of the training model Jesus used. Spectators see one, players do one, coaches teach one, and scouts recruit one (or more). The second row is the key to helping spectators become players, players become coaches, and coaches become scouts. The third row indicates the pitfalls of each position, where people may get hung up as they try to navigate to the next level. And the final row suggests the tools that may be helpful in the process. You may want to refer back to this matrix in each section that follows.

Introducing the Spectator

There's an old adage that says a football game is twenty-two desperately tired players being watched by twenty-two thousand spectators who desperately need to be out on the field. The Pareto principle puts a fine point onto that adage. Pareto observed that 20 percent of the people in any organization do approximately 80 percent of the work.[1] In the church, most generally conclude that these 20 percent are church leaders, but as we'll see later, in most churches the 20 percent actually represents very few leaders. However, most churches *do* have about 80 percent who seem

80 percent of most congregations are spectators.

content to sit and watch while the church "does its thing" week after week. But that's not the way it's supposed to be.

In the New Testament Paul writes that the church is the body of Christ, and everyone plays an important part in the work of the church (see 1 Cor. 12:12–31). However, in today's culture the problem that a "hand that doesn't want to be a hand" isn't the most pressing issue facing us. The big problem is that the hands, or the feet, or the knees, or the elbows really don't want to do or be *anything* other than spectators. A better description might be that these folks are consumer-Christians at best, willing to consume whatever the 20 percent are willing to offer.

In an effective church there is neither the "20 percent" nor the "80 percent"; there is just one body. The goal is for *every* member to identify their spiritual gifts, their talents, their skills, and most importantly, their passions, and put them to good use within the church and beyond the church. Therefore, one of the chief jobs of every church leader is to help spectators get out of the stands, off of the bench, and onto the ministry field. The effective church needs 80 percent of its people on the mission field.

From Spectator to Player

In terms of the Pareto principle, if the church spectators are the 80 percent then the players are the 20 percent. Particularly in a small church, it is easy to pick out the 20 percent. They're the ones who show up for everything, who have served on every committee, and who look very, very tired. If you catch them in a weak moment, they may tell you they are exhausted and wish some of the younger ones would step up so they could take a break. However, if the truth were known, most small churches are still small in part because their players rarely allow spectators to find a place on the playing field. We've discovered that if you can get beyond the redacted history, the odd spectator or two has already tried to break into the game only to discover that the players on the field either don't want to share their power or they're rather possessive about how "their" ministry is to be accomplished—and there's no room for innovation or change.

Perhaps the biggest misconception about players is the notion that this 20 percent is all leaders. Nothing could be further from the truth. Players are on the field. They *do*, not lead; they invest in practice and in playing; they rarely, if ever, invest in other players, let alone in spectators; and if we're completely honest, too many players prefer the superstar role over playing as a team. It's not that they don't want to share; it's that they have invested deeply in a ministry task rather than the ministry itself.

One of the historical realities about the role of players in traditional churches is that the committee system has perpetuated the rise of the Lone Star player. In many church systems, not only is the committee chair selected by a nominating committee, but the committee members are also nominated, voted on, and installed. In other churches, committee members rotate on and off only to be replaced by nominations from the nominating committee. In these and most other committee systems it is virtually impossible for a committee to function as a unified whole. Sure, ideally every member on the committee loves one another equally, respects one another completely, and trusts one another absolutely. If that were the case, the committee members could cooperate fully in the ministry and great things would be accomplished. However, we don't live in Fantasy Land. In the real world, committee members may not see eye to eye, and each brings their own baggage and ideas to the committee. This fosters either a competitive air, depending on the committee chair, or else a fatalistic culture that doesn't encourage an investment in the time and effort it takes to bring about change or compromise. The result is an ineffective committee that accomplishes ministry only when individuals take the initiative to do what needs to be done in spite of the rest of the committee. And who takes the field the lion's share of the time? Who else but the "leader," that is, the committee chair, who feels the weight of responsibility: "If it's going to get done, I'm going to have to do it myself."

Watching vs. Seeing

Referring to the training model mentioned in the matrix, the first step in moving a spectator into a player's position is to help them "see one" (they *see* someone *doing* ministry). However, far too many spectators just *see* and don't do anything about it. To see is a physical manifestation. Our eyes see much every day that we don't actually recognize, categorize, or even take notice of. The key, then, is to help spectators move from seeing to watching. *Watching* is an intentional act. When we watch something, we show interest in what we're seeing.

Consider the television. My (BTB) wife turns the television on first thing in the morning and then goes about her business getting ready for the day. Much of what is showing on the television goes completely unnoticed by her. However, every so often, she'll either see or hear something that catches her attention. At that moment, she stops what she's doing and "tunes in" to *watch*. If she gets *really* interested in the topic, she'll do an internet search, write down the recipe, or make a note to follow up later. In other words, to watch means to be engaged.

It isn't easy getting people to watch. Most leaders don't even try. Instead they'll ask any willing and able body to do virtually any task at hand. This is why we find accountants teaching junior high Sunday school for six months before they melt down, pull all their hair out, and run screaming from the church building never to be seen again. Therefore, it is vitally important to help spectators discover their personal passion in ministry.

Personal Passion

There are a number of spiritual gift and passion indicators available that can be used by the church. The Personal Ministry Assessment is an excellent tool for helping spectators identify their spiritual gifts, leadership styles, personal passions, and personality types.[2] Knowing what a spectator's passion is makes it easier for a leader to encourage them to *watch* instead of just see.

Once you have a spectator actually watching, it is a relatively easy task to help them become a player. In fact, many spectators will feel honored that they've been invited to become one of the players. However, before you start handing out jerseys, mitts, and playbooks, you'll want to make sure that each spectator fully understands what it means to be a player. The best way to do that is to share the vision and the expectations you have of them playing on the field. Remember: clear expectations are one of the marks of excellence in leadership.

One of the core needs of every human is the driving desire to make a difference. Too often people are recruited to serve in a position without having the benefit of understanding the real-world difference they could potentially make. For instance, rarely does a greeter understand the full potential of their service. Here's an example.

Before my wife and I (BTB) were married, we began looking for a church to attend. We were both United Methodists and were students at a United Methodist seminary. By chance, we visited Decatur Christian Church one Sunday morning. Before we even got to the front steps of the church, we were greeted by a tall, spry, older gentleman who introduced himself as Dean King and asked how we were. We introduced ourselves and responded with the requisite greeting, "And how are you?" He drew himself up, standing tall, and replied with a wink and a smile, "I feel like a King!" We spent the next five minutes chatting with Dean and learned a little bit about the church.

Clear expectations are one of the marks of excellence in leadership.

He then led us into the lobby and escorted us to an usher. "Give these two the best seats in the house" he began, and then dropped his voice and whispered just loud enough so we could hear, "and don't you charge them nothin'!" The usher's smile was almost painful and I suspect he'd heard that line before, but it was new to us and we couldn't help but grin. We tell this story often, because although the service was fine, we would not have returned to that church had it not been for Dean. And ultimately we became ordained ministers in the Christian Church . . . because of a greeter. In other words, a greeter can make a life-changing difference in someone's life.

When it comes to casting a vision to a prospective leader for how their work in a particular ministry could change lives, the most important thing to do is *look them in the eye*. You can tell if they have passion for the ministry you're describing by whether or not their eyes light up. When you pique someone's passion, invariably there is a physical manifestation. If their eyes don't light up, it's likely you haven't touched their passion. (Of course, there are those who never allow their emotions to get the best of them. In that case, you'll need to find some other measure.)

If you've made a bad guess and missed their passion, *do not recruit them as a player* until you discover what their passion really is. When people don't work within their passion, especially in a volunteer organization, they either burn out or become resentful. It is *always* better to leave a ministry position unfilled than to fill it with someone who lacks passion. When you see a spectator's eyes light up when you cast a vision, only *then* do you invite them to take the field. As you do, though, you need to be aware that there are two common pitfalls that trap rookie players far too often.

Common Rookie Pitfalls

The first pitfall is delegation without support. One might say this is actually a rookie mistake of an underdeveloped coach. In too many churches we've seen players disguised as coaches sending a player into the game as if the rookie player was a seasoned star pitcher. They hand them the ball, slap them once or twice on the shoulder, and tell them to "Go win one for the Gipper." Later, the wannabe-coach will wonder why their rookie player walked twelve batters, threw their arm out, and left the ministry field—or perhaps even the church. Like anything else we do, when we're new and fresh we make mistakes. We stumble around, we're unsure of ourselves, and we drop the ball at least once or twice. The only way to prevent a new player from becoming injured is to insist that they practice, practice, practice before anyone puts them in charge of a ministry.

When you cast a vision, do their eyes light up?

The second pitfall that costs many spectators their player status is that they become disengaged as time goes by. This happens for a couple of reasons. First, what may have seemed like the perfect position may quickly lose its luster after the first wild pitch under the big lights. Not everything that looks exciting remains exciting when you discover what really goes on behind the scenes. Second, there are those who believe that raw passion and desire alone guarantee success; however, it's been said that it takes fifteen years of hard work to become an overnight success. Although most spectators can become star players rather quickly if they're working within their passion, some simply don't have what it takes to endure the necessary practice. Of course, some seek positions simply because they want the power and control associated with that position—but that's a problem and a pitfall for another book.

The solution to these pitfalls is for the leader to remain engaged with the rookie player and not abdicate follow-up. A good coach never leaves the dugout while their players are in the game, and an effective leader mentors and coaches on a continuing basis. As we hope you've learned through this book, players and coaches—even experienced coaches—benefit from ongoing coaching. Indeed, players who become effective coaches not only coach, they insist on having a coach.

From Player to Coach

If players represent the 20 percent, then coaches represent approximately 20 percent of the 20 percent (see the diagram below). That means in a church of one hundred in worship there are approximately twenty players, and of those twenty players there are only four coaches. In other words, as a congregational leader you will need to be very selective about the players you recruit as potential coaches.

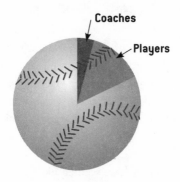

There is probably no more difficult job in the church than moving a player into the role of a leader, let alone a coach or scout. For one, many players have never seen a real-life example of a leader in action. In many churches, even the pastors they've seen have been players rather than leaders or coaches. Certainly, many of these so-called leaders have found it easier to just do what needs to get done rather than depending on others. Perhaps they've been burned by those who have promised to get something done but didn't, or worse who *did* get it done but did it so badly that it was an embarrassment both to the pastor and the church. You only have to be called on the carpet once or twice for the failings of someone you had counted on before you become gun-shy and conclude that it's easier and better to do it yourself.

Without effective models of leaders in the church, no one should be surprised how difficult it is to train a player to become an effective leader. However, if you are a committed leader who not only understands what a leader is but also what a leader does, and puts that into practice, then it's possible to help your players go to the next level. But leaders must value getting ministry done through others more than themselves.

Leaders have to model the game for apprentices.

Apprenticeship Basics

When it comes to helping a player move into leadership, the first step is to take them under your wing as an apprentice so you can coach and mentor them. Since it is the rare player who has actually seen a real church leader in action, it will be critical for them to watch you closely and learn from you.

There are three basic practices of apprenticeship: model, mentor, and multiply. Formal modeling can only take place when a player has become an apprentice—in other words, after they have agreed to become a leader. Before you invest in this mentoring process you'll want to be as sure as you can be that the player is committed to the ministry they are engaged in, as well as committed to creating a legacy beyond themselves. It is essential to help your prospective leader understand that their primary job will be to raise up other players and leaders in order to accomplish the ministry tasks. In other words, their main job is to remove themself from direct hands-on ministry. You can assure them they'll still be busy, but their ministry will be helping others to succeed.

Once a player has agreed to be apprenticed as a leader, the next step is simply to model what you want them to do. You don't have to do their job for them, at least in terms of recruiting new players and leaders on their behalf. However, they will need to *watch* you recruit, train, and coach new players and leaders. You will also have to be careful not to fall into the trap of running onto the field to carry the ball—that is, to be a player-coach. Remember, they will be watching you closely. You'll need to model effective leadership, and particularly how to delegate/empower, follow up, and coach.

For example, suppose you need a skit performed at an upcoming worship service to serve as a sermon illustration. With your apprentice at your side, you approach one of your members who is a high school drama teacher. While you are casting the vision for the skit, the teacher's eyes light up and you move from visioning into a recruiting conversation. Once they've accepted, you verify the details and ensure they understand your expectations of what needs to be done and by when. You end the conversation by making a checkup appointment well in advance of the deadline. When the appointment time rolls around, you again take your apprentice. During the appointment, you practice good coaching techniques by asking questions, helping set goals, and holding the teacher accountable for reaching their goals. As per your custom, you end the checkup appointment by scheduling an additional appointment. In our example, this final meeting would be scheduled a week before the performance. Your apprentice would join you for this final appointment as well, and your conversation with the teacher would primarily revolve around the successful completion of their goals. In the end, if you have recruited and coached well, the skit would be performed without a hitch and your apprentice would have witnessed firsthand what it means to lead effectively.

As your apprentice sees successful leadership practices, it becomes time for you to mentor them specifically toward leadership. The first step in that training is to teach them to delegate effectively. Far too often in the church, delegation has meant asking a volunteer to do something, handing them a book or a manual, and sending them onto the playing field with no further follow-up. In general, the thought seems to be that they will return to seek help if and when they need it; however, in our independent Western culture many have embraced the mistaken notion that asking for help is a sign of weakness at best, and incompetence at worst. Therefore, instead of asking for help, most players simply continue to struggle on, even when they reach an impasse, and would rather give up and quit than ask for assistance. Delegation without follow-up is a recipe for failure and a sign of poor leadership.

Successful mentoring will mean providing your apprentice with multiple short-term opportunities to practice their new skills. As you coach them, help them break down the ministry into short-term tasks or events. Each of these will provide an opportunity to coach them through the goal-setting process. Make sure you help them celebrate as they reach their goals through the hands and feet of those they are leading.

Potential Pitfalls

As you work with your apprentice, be aware of the two most common pitfalls. First, many players are married to "their way" and will insist on imposing their "how-tos" on their recruited players and leaders. This is a hard habit to break, and you will need to be diligent as you coach your apprentice to ensure they have the ability to give their ministry team some creative latitude.

The second and most detrimental pitfall is when the leader doesn't trust the player and/or the team. There are two solutions to the trust issue. To begin with, help create a culture where it's okay to take a risk and fail. In most cases, we take success *way* too seriously. This stifles creativity and contributes to a congregation's inability to remain relevant to the wider community. "We've always done it this way" is an indication that ministry is in danger of being outdated, outmoded, irrelevant, and obsolete. When a culture encourages opportunities to risk and fail, it is easier to celebrate success and embrace trust.[3] The second solution to trust issues provides us with an important leadership lesson. This solution begins with the question: "Why would you put someone in a position if you didn't trust them?" If the answer is "We needed a warm body to do a task," then the issue isn't about trust—it's about poor leadership and poor recruiting. *Never* put someone that you must count on into a position when you aren't nearly certain that they: (1) can do the job, (2) *want* to do the job, and (3) are trustworthy. Remember, passion is just about everything. Putting someone in a ministry position when their eyes *don't* light up is usually a costly mistake. Help your apprentice to recruit only those they can trust and then help them to actually trust them. The one caveat is for an untested player, someone who's new to the church or to your circle of influence. In these cases it's important to switch to delegation mode (see the accountability sections in chapters 12 and 13 for more).

Players have moved to the coaching level when they have learned to effectively delegate/empower and coach other players to do the ministry tasks they once accomplished on their own. When they have reached this level, they have become real leaders. Heaven knows the church needs more leaders; however, what the church needs even more than leaders are effective leaders who can scout future leaders. And that's the next step.

From Coach to Scout

Not everyone has the aptitude and/or interest to become an effective coach, let alone an accomplished scout. A great scout not only identifies spectators who are ready to become players, but they can spot a player who would make an effective coach as well.

There are only two effective ways to become an effective scout. The first is through relationships, relationships, relationships. Get to know your players well. Listen to their passions. Watch what they do. Mentor them well, coach them better, and look for multiplication. When you see someone multiplying players themselves, that's a pretty good indication they'd make a good candidate. The second way is simply through experience. The more time you spend watching players doing ministry, the better you'll become at noticing who's a viable coaching candidate and who isn't. Note the key word in that sentence: *watching*. Just like a spectator, if you don't take the time to move from seeing to watching it's unlikely you'll make the leap to the next level. In this case it's not keeping your eye on the ball—it's keeping your eye on the players.

According to the Scriptures there should be no end to the number of players in our congregation—we are all members of the body of Christ and we all have our part to play. Helping players become effective leaders is one of the most difficult tasks placed upon us. From all appearances, at the end of Jesus's ministry as recorded in the Gospels, it seemed he'd failed miserably as a leader. His apprentice-leaders scattered and went into hiding. Indeed, it took an infusion of the Holy Spirit to propel his little band of spectators back onto the playing field and then onto the sidelines as leader-coaches. All that's to say if Jesus had a hard time raising up effective future leaders, don't be discouraged if at first you don't succeed! But as the axiom says, "Try, try again," and pray that the Holy Spirit will intervene . . . because you know, the Spirit just might.

Conclusion

From Here to There

We realize that we've covered a lot of ground, thrown a lot at you, and in some places haven't been as eloquent or expansive as we could have been. Staffing for an effective church is a lot more like an art than a skill, and yet we believe every church leader, every staff member, and every lead pastor can move from crayons to oil painting with diligence, with practice, and perhaps most importantly, with a coach.

If you're going to take seriously our call to lead an effective church, you have difficult decisions before you. Starting to hold your staff accountable for results, let alone holding volunteer leaders accountable, will put you on the hot seat with your board. We've found that few churches take accountability seriously, and even fewer church leaders take the time to communicate clear expectations—the foundation for accountability. And never mind how difficult it will be to remove ineffective staff members and volunteer leaders. If you want to start a war, just mention the possibility of retiring the church secretary who's been with the church since it was chartered but who still doesn't understand why anyone would bother with email. We understand how difficult it will be to change your church's culture, but we hope you understand that if it doesn't change, the chances of becoming an effective church are zip.

And so let us leave you with a list of ponderables. Refer to this list as you travel the leadership journey to help stay on track. Each question includes a chapter reference so you can refresh your memory as needed. Consider each question as you traverse TP1 to TP4. Reflect on them. Weigh the implications. Measure them against the mission of the church and against your personal life mission. Dream about what the church could become as it increases its effectiveness. And don't forget that we're here for you. We're pulling for you—we're all in this together, as Red Green would say.

Ask yourself:

- Is the primary role of your staff to care for people and programs, or to equip and send effective disciples? (ch. 2)
- Are you spending enough time networking with the unchurched? (ch. 4, 10, 12)
- Are all four core processes adequately being taken care of? (ch. 3)
- Do first-time visitors feel like "welcome guests" or "hot commodities"? (ch. 5)
- Are first-time guests personally contacted within twenty-four hours of their visit? (ch. 5)
- Are your church's ministries focused on in-reach or outreach? (ch. 7)
- Are your leaders "willing and able" or "passionate and unstoppable"? (ch. 8)
- Is your church organization structure scalable as-is for double your current size? Triple? Even larger? (ch. 8)
- Is each program staff person regularly raising up new leaders? (ch. 8)
- Have you set clear expectations for all of your staff? (ch. 13)
- Do you hold your staff accountable for doing what is expected? (ch. 12, 13)
- Are all the staff self-starters and empowered to work on their own? (ch. 13, 14)
- Do you spend the necessary time to coach your staff? (ch. 8, 13)
- Have you identified your four key leaders who will be responsible for the four core processes? (ch. 3–7)
- Do you have any staff members that are holding you back? (ch. 12, 13)

- Are your staff meetings "To Do" or "To Be" conversations? (ch. 7, 16)
- What systems do you have in place to assimilate people and close the back door? (ch. 5, 15)
- Do you have adequate space for your cars and crowds? (ch. 15)
- Are you prepared to take the worship and children's experience to the next level? (ch. 15)
- Are your "leaders" players or coaches? (ch. 8, 17)

Now it's time to take the risk and begin the transition from a "Y'all come" attractional church to a "Let's go to them" missional church. God and the world are waiting. How long can you resist?

Coaching & Mentoring Notes

Apprentice/Leader: _____

Date: _____

Check-in: _____

Goal

Reality

Options/Next Steps

Resources

Check Out

Next Appointment: _____

Notes

Chapter 1 Every Church Is Missional, or It Isn't a Church

1. Attractional churches are those that depend on the unchurched finding their way into the church building rather than depending on the members being the church in the community. The unspoken motto of attractional churches is "Y'all come!" whereas the spoken motto for the incarnational church is "We all go!"

Chapter 2 The Context for Everything

1. J. D. Payne, "Global Migration in the United States and Canada," *Great Commission Research Journal* 2:1 (Summer 2010): 23–25.

2. According to Crosswalk, only 40 percent of Americans attend worship and only 10 percent attend church on a weekly basis (http://www.crosswalk. com/1396537/). However, many statisticians suggest that only 20 percent of Americans actually attend worship.

3. In 1948, when Gallup began tracking religious identification, the percentage who claimed to be Christian was 91 percent (http://www.gallup.com/poll/117409/ easter-smaller-percentage-americans-christian.aspx). Today fewer than 75 percent of Americans claim to be Christian; 15 percent claim no religious affiliation at all, and that number is growing every year. In 1972, Gallup measured 5 percent with "no religion." According to CNN, "America is a less Christian nation than it was 20 years ago, and Christianity is not losing out to other religions, but primarily to a rejection of religion altogether." (http://www.cnn.com/2009/LIVING/ wayoflife/03/09/us.religion.less.christian/).

4. David Olson, *The American Church in Crisis* (Grand Rapids: Zondervan, 2008), 175.

Chapter 4 Process One

1. See Bill Tenny-Brittian, "Holiday Hand-Offs," *Net Results* (Nov–Dec 2007), for an article on the importance and use of hand-offs.

2. See ideas for Fishing Pool events and other ways to connect with the unchurched at http://bit.ly/FishingPool.

3. Charles Arn, *Heartbeat* (Maitland, FL: Xulon Press, 2011).

4. For more on this campaign, see our workbook "I Love My Church Day" at http://EffectiveChurch.com/LoveMyChurch.

Chapter 5 Process Two

1. Ush (v.): The act of helping people to the best seats in the house, rather than being a human bulletin dispenser. Ushers ask every person who passes through their door, "Do you have a seating preference?" Sure, the "regulars" will roll their eyes the first couple of weeks, but guests just won't be able to do anything but marvel at the church's over-the-top welcome and class.

2. Unfortunately, the word *contemporary* carries a lot of baggage in terms of worship style. In many if not most churches we work with, contemporary is synonymous with Baby Boomer worship (keyboard and guitar-driven choruses). For our purposes, when we use the word *indigenous* to describe a worship style, please recognize we mean any style of worship that is nontraditional.

3. For information on how to increase the number of guests who provide contact information, see www.VisitorFollowUp.net.

4. Don't automatically presume that a drop-in visit will be an unwanted intrusion, even if you've "asked around" and heard negative responses. Instead, try the two-minute drop-off drill for six months to a year and keep track of the responses, specifically the percentage of first-time guests who return. If you've experienced a significant increase, don't stop.

5. Missional communities are small groups of Christians who spend most of their time in the community and may or may not be connected with a local congregation. They carry on all the functions of a church, including worship and service in the community, but aren't necessarily part of a local church.

6. For more information on how to do this, see Bill Easum and John Atkinson, *Go Big with Small Groups* (Abingdon Press, 2007).

7. Larry Osborne, *Sticky Church* (Grand Rapids: Zondervan, 2008).

Chapter 7 Process Four

1. One of the best websites to give you a list of practical deed ministries for a community is http://www.servantevangelism.com/matrix/matrix.htm.

2. Bill Easum and Dave Travis, *Beyond the Box* (Loveland, CO: Group Publishing, 2003).

3. An excellent book on this subject is Dino Rizzo, *Servolution* (Grand Rapids: Zondervan, 2009).

Chapter 8 Leadership Multiplication

1. For more on the midwife metaphor see Bill Easum, *Leadership On the Other Side* (Nashville: Abingdon Press, 2000).

2. Dave Ferguson and Jon Ferguson, *Exponential* (Grand Rapids: Zondervan, 2010).

3. See Bill Tenny-Brittian, *The Apprentice Workbook* (Charleston, SC: BookSurge, 2007), for an effective small group mentoring process.

Chapter 10 The Leadership Journey for the Solo Pastor and the Smaller Church

1. If your congregation has had more than three or four successive pastors who have failed to grow the church, the odds are the issue isn't pastoral leadership. In these cases it is virtually impossible to grow a church without significant outside help. We recommend calling a qualified church consultant to help. See www.ChurchConsultations.com for helpful advice on getting a church consultant.

2. See chapter 3 in Bill Easum and Bill Tenny-Brittian, *Ministry in Hard Times* (Nashville: Abingdon Press, 2010).

3. See Ken Ham et al., *Already Gone: Why Your Kids Will Leave Church and What You Can Do to Stop It* (Green Forest, AR: New Leaf Publishing, 2009).

Chapter 11 The Leadership Journey for the Lead Pastor

1. We are indebted to Ram Charan, Stephen Drotter, and James Noel, the authors of *Leadership Pipeline* (San Francisco: Jossey-Bass, 2001), for their work in developing a business model for these three changes in leadership. We have taken their three basic changes and applied them to the changes that must take place in the life of a pastor and staff.

2. We are indebted to Bob Roberts for the use of this term. For more information visit http://www.glocal.net/.

Chapter 13 The Journey through Transition Point Two

1. For a detailed interview and hiring process, see chapter 8 in Bill Easum, *Unfreezing Moves* (Nashville: Abingdon Press, 2001).

2. Although this feedback form is effective in the short term, we recommend an annual 360 for every ministry leader when possible in order to provide a broader perspective of the leader's effectiveness. The 360 evaluation is fast becoming the standard of leadership evaluations in both the for- and non-profit worlds.

It provides feedback from more than just the immediate supervisor, including parallel feedback from co-workers, those the leader supervises, team members, and even colleagues and clients.

Chapter 14 The Journey through Transition Point Three

1. Taken from Warren Bennis and Joan Goldsmith, *Learning to Lead: A Workbook on Becoming a Leader*, 4th ed. (New York: Basic Books, 2010).

Chapter 15 The Journey through Transition Point Four

1. For more information see Dave Ferguson, Eric Bramlett, and Jon Ferguson, *The Big Idea* (Grand Rapids: Zondervan, 2007).

2. Aviva Lucas Gutnick et al., "Always Connected," Joan Ganz Cooney Center, March 2011, http://joanganzcooneycenter.org/Reports-28.html.

3. To see one of the best children's ministries visit Bay Area Fellowship in Corpus Christi, Texas. If you can't do that, visit them online to see what they offer at www.bayareafellowship.com.

4. Dan Reaves, personal interview, 2005.

Chapter 16 Staffing Basics

1. Bill Easum, *Unfreezing Moves*, chap. 8.

2. For more information visit Birkman International, Inc. at http://www.birkman.com.

Chapter 17 The Player-Coach Dilemma

1. See Richard Kock, *The 80/20 Principle* (New York: Doubleday, 1998).

2. Bill Tenny-Brittian and Kris Tenny-Brittian, "The Personal Ministry Assessment," http://EffectiveChurch.com/PMA.

3. A great new book on adventure and risk taking is *The Faith of Leap* by Alan Hirsch and Michael Frost (Grand Rapids: Baker, 2011).